MICHAEL COOPER

COLLINS
CHILDREN'S
ATLAS

COLLINS

Our World . . 6-15

An introduction to the planet Earth, its position and movement in space, its measurement, its formation and structure, its climate; the drifting of its continents – and the changes wrought by rivers, winds, ice, oceans – and man.

Maps 17-59

Original world maps showing geological features as well as country boundaries, cities and major towns.

To/ Nerosh . J

Nerosh JEYAKUMARAN, book

FROM

PAPA

Cartography
MALCOLM PORTER

Editor
MICHAEL COOPER

Text
KEITH LYE
DAVID ROSS

Illustrations
MIKE ATKINSON
MIKE SAUNDERS

First published by Granada Publishing 1985
Revised edition published by
William Collins Sons & Co Ltd 1989
This impression 1990
© William Collins Sons & Co Ltd
Reprinted in 1991

Material in the Our World and Flags section of this book
has previously been published in the Granada Guide to
Flags 1981 and to Planet Earth 1983

The Publishers would like to thank the Flag Institute for
the up-to-date information on flags contained in this Atlas.

British Library Cataloguing in Publication Data available.
ISBN 0-00-190071-4 (HB)
ISBN 0-00-190072-2 (PB)

Printed in Great Britain by HarperCollins Manufacturing, Glasgow

Flags 61-77

The flags of nations and states are illustrated with a description of their origins, development and symbolism. The populations and sizes of the countries are also given.

Index 79-94

A comprehensive index to all three sections: Our World, Maps and Flags.

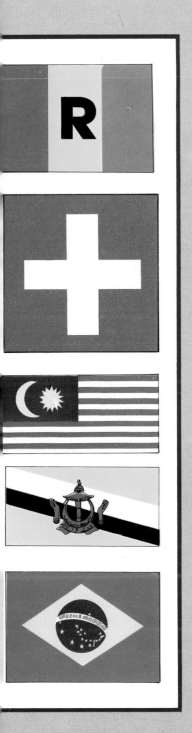

OUR WORLD

The Earth is one of nine planets that rotate around the Sun in the Solar System. The Earth is only a tiny speck in space. The Sun's diameter is 109 times that of the Earth. And the Sun is only a medium-sized star, one of about 100,000 in the Milky Way galaxy. Some of these stars may have planets much like our Earth orbiting around them.

The Earth is a terrestrial planet – that is, it is dense and rocky, like Mars, Mercury, Pluto and Venus. Jupiter, Neptune, Saturn and Uranus are much larger, low-density balls of gas.

People once thought that the Earth was flat. But photographs taken from space show that it is round. It is not a perfect sphere. It bulges out slightly at the equator and is flattened at the poles. The polar diameter, joining the North and South poles via the centre of the Earth is 12,713 km long. The diameter across the equator is 43 km longer.

The Earth looks blue from space, because water covers about 71 per cent of the planet's surface. Water is one of the three parts of the Earth. It is called the *hydrosphere*. The other parts are the *lithosphere* (the rocks) and the *atmosphere* (the air around the Earth). The Earth is forever changing. The oceans are being widened or made smaller by movements in the rocks under the Earth's crust. The lithosphere changes as volcanoes create new rocks and surface rocks are worn away. The atmosphere is always on the move, making the weather change from day to day. Life on Earth has also changed throughout a 4600 million-year-long history.

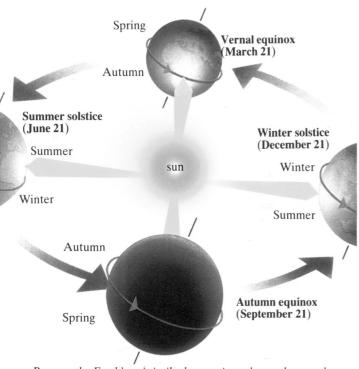

Because the Earth's axis is tilted, sometimes the northern and sometimes the southern hemisphere leans towards the Sun. The seasons in the two hemispheres are opposite to each other.

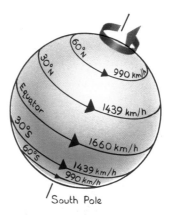

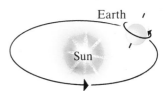

Above: The Earth takes about 365¼ days to make one complete journey around the Sun. Left: The Earth spins like a top once every 24 hours. The speed at which the Earth rotates decreases away from the equator.

Earth Time

The Earth is racing through space in three ways. First, the entire Solar System is swinging around the centre of the Milky Way galaxy at a speed of 69,200 km/h. Second, the Earth rotates around the Sun at an average speed of 106,200 km/h, taking one *solar year* (365 days, 5 hours, 48 minutes and 46 seconds) to complete the journey. A solar year is about one-fourth of a day more than the calendar year of 365 days. This extra time is allowed for on calendars

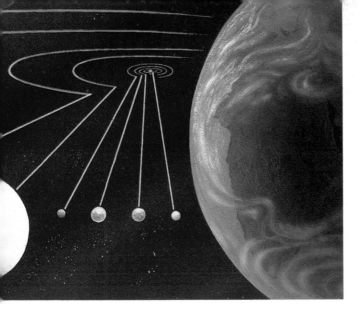

The planets of the Solar System (from left to right): Pluto, Neptune, Uranus, Saturn, Jupiter, Mars, Earth, Venus and Mercury. Right: The Earth as seen from space.

by having a leap year of 366 days every four years. The Earth also spins on its axis in one *mean solar day* (24 hours). The axis is the imaginary line joining the North and South poles. As the Earth spins, the Sun appears to move across the sky from the east, where it rises, to the west, where it sets.

Because the Earth's axis is tilted by 23½°, the northern and southern hemispheres experience seasons. On March 21, the *vernal equinox*, the Sun is overhead at the equator and its heat is evenly distributed. But after March 21, as the Earth rotates, the northern hemisphere starts to tilt towards the Sun. On June 21, the *summer solstice*, the Sun is overhead at the Tropic of Cancer (latitude 23½° North) and the northern hemisphere gets more heat than the southern. After June 21, the northern hemisphere gradually tilts away from the Sun. On September 23, the *autumn equinox*, the Sun is overhead at the equator. The southern hemisphere then tilts towards the Sun. On December 21, the *winter solstice*, the Sun is overhead at the Tropic of Capricorn (23½° South), where it is summer.

Lines of latitude are imaginary lines around the Earth that are parallel to the equator, which is 0°. The North Pole is latitude 90° North and the South Pole is 90° South. The latitude of any other point is the angle formed at the centre of the Earth between the point and the equator. Lines of longitude, or meridians, are measured either 180° east, or 180° west of the prime meridian, which is 0° longitude.

Measuring the Earth

The position of any place on Earth is described by two measurements, latitude and longitude. Lines of latitude and longitude appear on maps, which show part or all of the Earth's surface on a flat piece of paper. The latitude of a place is a measurement of how far it is north or south of the equator – that is, between 0° latitude (the equator) and 90° North (the North Pole) or 90° South (the South Pole). The distance from the equator to one of the poles is about 10,002 km, so 1° of latitude is 111 km.

The longitude of a place is a measurement of how far the place is east or west of the prime meridian, or 0° longitude. The prime meridian runs from the North Pole to the South Pole through the former Royal Astronomical Observatory at Greenwich, London. At the equator, 1° of longitude is 111 km. At the poles, it is zero, because all the lines meet there.

The line of longitude 180° West is the same as 180° East. This line of longitude is the International Date Line. If you travel from east to west across this line, you lose a whole day. But if you travel from west to east, you gain a day. This happens because 15° of longitude represent one hour of time as the Earth spins on its axis. Hence, if you travel east of Greenwich, you must advance your clock by one hour for every 15° of longitude, so that at 180° East, the time is 12 hours *ahead* of Greenwich. Travelling west, you put your clock back by one hour for every 15° of longitude. Hence, at 180° West, the time is 12 hours *behind* Greenwich. This means that the time difference between two points on either side of the International Date Line is 24 hours.

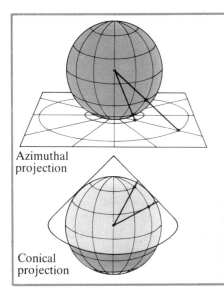

MAP PROJECTIONS Curved surfaces cannot be shown accurately on a flat map. Perspective map projections are made by imagining the Earth as a glass globe with a light at its centre. Shadows of lines of latitude and longitude are cast onto paper, as in the azimuthal and conical projections shown here. Perspective map projections are often adjusted to reduce the amount of distortion.

Azimuthal projection

Conical projection

Formation of the Earth

Scientists have put forward several theories to explain the origin of the Solar System. Some think that it was formed from material pulled away from the Sun when a star passed near it. Others consider that the Sun was once extremely large. As it spun around, it threw out gases and dust into a disc. This material formed into planets. But most scientists think that the Solar System formed from a huge cloud of dust and gas, the remains of exploded stars. Material in this cloud was drawn by gravity to the centre to form the Sun. The rest of the material was drawn into blobs around 4600 million years ago. These blobs developed into planets.

The new-born Earth was fiercely hot. Heavy substances sank towards the centre of the molten body. Lighter substances were thrown upwards by volcanic explosions which released gases and water vapour from the rocks. The water vapour formed clouds and heavy rain lashed the blazing surface. Slowly, the surface hardened to form a thin crust. Occasionally, molten rocks burst through the crust in volcanoes.

The Earth is now divided into three main zones: the crust, mantle and core. The crust reaches a maximum depth of 60–70 km under mountain ranges. The oceanic crust, however, is only about 6 km thick. The crust consists mostly of light materials. It rests upon the mostly solid, 2900-km-thick mantle, where the rocks are much denser (heavier). The densest zone, however, is the core, which has a diameter of about 6920 km. The outer part of the core is probably molten, and the inner core solid.

The Earth is covered by a hard, thin crust. Beneath the crust is the thick, dense mantle. The Earth's core is divided into a liquid outer core and a solid inner core.

Igneous Rocks

Minerals are homogeneous substances. This means that they have a definite chemical composition and that any part of a mineral is exactly the same as any other part. Rocks consist of minerals, but the amounts of minerals in a rock vary from one sample to another. This means that rocks do not have a definite chemical composition.

There are three main kinds of rocks: igneous rocks, sedimentary rocks and metamorphic rocks. Igneous rocks are formed from magma. Magma is molten rock that has risen up through the Earth's crust.

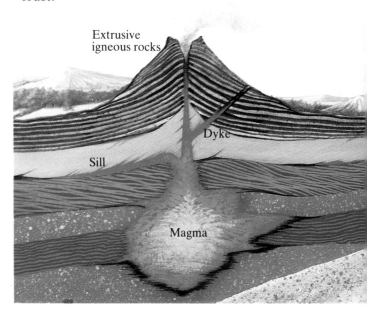

Igneous rocks form in several ways. The common rock basalt is hardened lava. Granite forms from molten rock that has hardened well below the surface. Obsidian, or volcanic glass, forms on the surface from magma that cools rapidly in the air.

Sedimentary and Metamorphic Rocks

Many sedimentary rocks are made up of worn fragments of rock. These fragments, including pebbles, sand and mud, are swept into lakes and seas by rivers. There they pile up in layers. The layers, or *strata*, are compressed and the grains of sand and mud are cemented together by minerals deposited by seeping water. Such rocks are called *clastic* rocks. They include conglomerates, sandstones, mudstones and shales.

Metamorphic rocks are igneous or sedimentary rocks that have been changed by great heat, pressure or chemical action. Metamorphic rocks include marble, which was formerly limestone, slate, which was originally shale, mudstone or tuff, and quartzite, which formed from quartz sandstones.

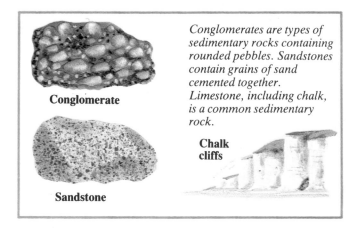

Conglomerates are types of sedimentary rocks containing rounded pebbles. Sandstones contain grains of sand cemented together. Limestone, including chalk, is a common sedimentary rock.

Conglomerate

Sandstone

Chalk cliffs

Obsidian   Basalt   Granite

Intrusive igneous rocks

Climate and Vegetation

Climate is the average, or usual, weather of a place. It is based mainly on average temperatures and rainfall. One major factor affecting climate is latitude – that is, how near the place is to the tropics or polar regions. But other factors, such as the height of the land, are important. Snow-capped mountain peaks on the equator have a polar climate. Nearness to the sea also affects climate. For example, northern Norway is within the Arctic Circle, but its coasts are warmed by an ocean current that flows across the Atlantic Ocean from the Caribbean Sea. By contrast, places at the hearts of continents have severe climates.

There are several types of climate. Tropical climates include hot and wet equatorial regions, with rain all the year round. This climate supports dense forests, like those in the Amazon and Zaïre basins. Around the forests are hot areas with a marked dry season. These areas contain light forests or savanna (grassland). The savanna merges in parts of the horse latitude zones into hot deserts.

Temperate zones range from Mediterranean lands with hot, dry summers and cool, moist winters, to the cool coniferous forest regions of the northern hemisphere. Beyond the coniferous forests is the treeless tundra with its long winters. And beyond the tundra are the snow-covered polar lands.

The climate determines the vegetation and animal life of a region. But people can live comfortably anywhere, if their homes are equipped with central heating and air conditioning.

Other sedimentary rocks are of organic origin. Organic rocks consist mostly of the remains of once-living things. For example, coal consists of the remains of ancient swamp plants and some limestones are composed of the shells of sea creatures.

Many sedimentary rocks form in seas from material worn from the land. Rivers transport the sediment to the sea.

Sand and pebbles

Sand

Mud

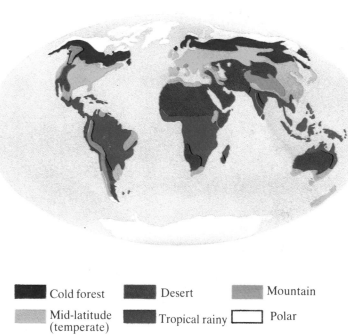

■ Cold forest	■ Desert	■ Mountain
■ Mid-latitude (temperate)	■ Tropical rainy	□ Polar

The Oceans

A better name for our planet would be 'Water' or 'Ocean', because oceans cover 71 per cent of the globe. Until recently, little was known about the world beneath the waves, but in the last 30 to 40 years, the study of the oceans has become a major science. Large parts of the oceans have been mapped and scientists have visited the deepest parts of the oceans in vessels called bathyscaphes and bathyspheres. We now realize that the oceans are a great storehouse of food and minerals for the future.

Left: If you look at a globe, you will find views that include most of the world's land masses, such as the view shown below. But another view is dominated by the largest of the oceans, the Pacific. This view is sometimes called the water hemisphere. The oceans cover about 71 per cent of the Earth's surface.

The oceans are divided into three main zones: the continental shelves, the continental slopes, and the abyss. The continental shelves are gently sloping areas near the continents. Some continental shelves, such as that off western Europe, extend far out to sea. Others, such as that off the western coast of South America, are narrow. The shelves end at the continental slopes, which plunge sharply down to the abyss. The top of the continental slope is the true edge of the continental land masses.

The abyss contains plains, long mountain ranges, called oceanic ridges, and volcanic mountains, some of which form islands. The volcano Mauna Kea, in Hawaii, can claim to be the world's highest mountain. It rises 10,023 metres from the ocean floor, although only 4204 metres are above sea level. The average depth of the oceans is about 3550 metres, but the ocean trenches are much deeper. A record depth of 11,033 metres has been measured in the Marianas Trench in the Pacific Ocean.

The oceans are youthful features in geological terms. Although rocks more than 3500 million years old have been found on land, no rocks on the ocean bed are more than 200 million years old.

The oceans are interconnected and contain nearly 1300 million cubic kilometres of water. This is more than 97 per cent of the world's water. Most of the remainder is locked in ice sheets.

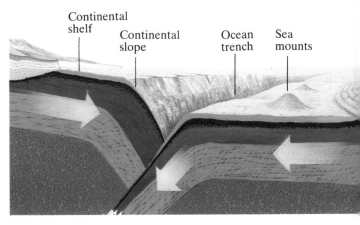

The ocean bed has varied scenery, with volcanic mountains and islands, ocean trenches, plains, mountain ranges and canyons.

The Changing Earth

In one person's lifetime, the land may not appear to change much. In fact, it is changing all the time. Some changes are dramatic, as when Mount St Helens erupted in the USA in 1980, killing 65 people in an explosion that ripped about 425 metres from the top of the volcano. Most changes, however, are slow. They include the natural erosion of the land and the slow drifting of the continents.

Continents have been on the move for millions of years. But the theory of continental drift has been accepted by most scientists for barely 20 years. Evidence for continental drift can be seen on a world map, where North and South America look as though they would fit against Europe and Africa like pieces in a giant jigsaw. The fit is even better if, instead of the coasts, the edges of the continental shelves, the true edges of the continents, are placed together. Other evidence for drift comes from the studies of rocks and fossils.

Scientists now believe that, 200 million years ago, there was only one continent. They call this continent Pangaea. Pangaea gradually broke apart and the continents slowly moved, at rates between one and ten centimetres a year, to their present positions. Continental drift continues today. For example, the Atlantic Ocean is still getting wider, while the Mediterranean Sea is closing up.

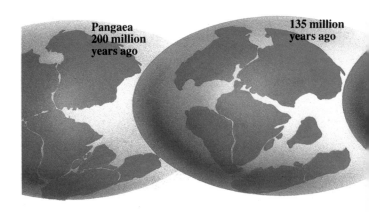

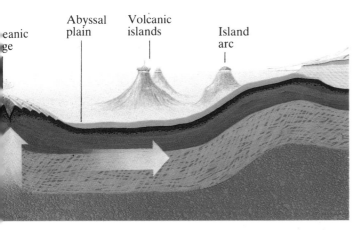

Abyssal plain — Volcanic islands — Island arc — ...eanic ...ge

The Earth's crust is split into large, rigid sections called *tectonic plates*. These consist of continents, continental shelves and the ocean crust that also underlies the continents. The plates rest on the dense mantle. In the upper mantle, heat causes semi-fluid rock to rise. Just beneath the plates, the rocks spread outwards until, finally, they cool and sink. These movements are called *convection currents*. They occur directly under the ocean ridges, which are plate edges. As the hot rocks rise and spread outwards, they pull the plates along with them. Hot magma plugs the gap as the plates move apart and then cools to become crustal rock.

The map shows that the Earth's crust is cracked into a series of plates, both large and small. These plates are continually moving.

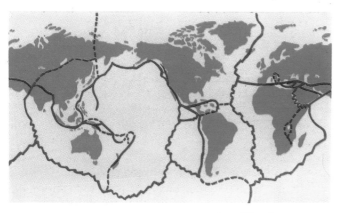

Ocean spreading occurs along the ocean ridges. The plates on either side of the ridges are pulled apart by convection currents in the upper mantle. The gaps are filled by volcanic rock.

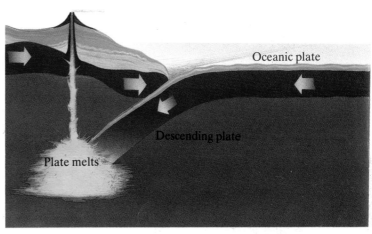

Oceanic plate

Descending plate

Plate melts

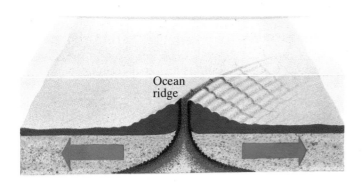

Ocean ridge

These maps show how the oceans formed as the continents drifted apart in the last 200 million years. The continents were formerly joined in a super-continent called Pangaea.

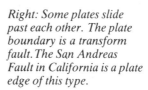

When two plates push against each other, one slides down beneath the other. As it descends, the edge of the plate melts. The melted rock, or magma, may rise to the Earth's surface through volcanoes.

Right: Some plates slide past each other. The plate boundary is a transform fault. The San Andreas Fault in California is a plate edge of this type.

New crustal rock is, therefore, being created along the ocean ridges. Elsewhere, crustal rock is being destroyed. The destruction takes place under the deep ocean trenches where one plate is forced down beneath another. As the plate descends, friction, pressure and heat melt the edge of the plate. This creates magma, which may then rise through volcanoes in the overlying plate.

Ocean ridges and trenches are two of the three kinds of plate edges. The third is the transform fault. Along these faults (cracks), the plates move jerkily alongside each other. Plate edges are associated with earthquakes and volcanic activity. The study of plate movements has helped geologists to explain how these phenomena occur.

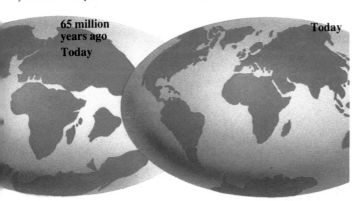

65 million years ago
Today
Today

11

Earthquakes

Earthquakes are caused by shock waves that travel through the Earth's crust. They may be generated by landslides, explosions or volcanic eruptions, but most result from sudden movements along faults in the rocks. Earthquakes can occur anywhere, although the most destructive ones strike near plate edges.

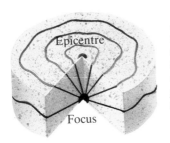

Left: The focus is the place where an earthquake originates. The point on the surface above the focus is the epicentre. Isoseismal lines join points with the same degree of shock.

Plate movements are never smooth. For example, the plate edges along transform faults become jammed. The pressure slowly mounts over a number of years. Suddenly the jammed rocks snap and the plates jerk forward, triggering off an earthquake.

An average of 10,000 earthquakes are recorded every year. Most of them have a low *magnitude* (strength), but around 10 cause loss of life and destruction of property. In 1556, a record number of about 800,000 people perished in a terrible earthquake in China. Earthquakes may cause fires, started by broken gas pipes and electrical short-circuits. Scientists are still trying to find accurate ways of forecasting earthquakes.

Volcanoes

Volcanoes are the outlets for hot magma from the Earth's interior. Most of the world's 530 or so active volcanoes are situated near plate edges, notably along the ocean ridges and near the *subduction zones*, where one plate is descending beneath another. The descending plate melts and creates a reservoir of magma. Some volcanoes, like those in Hawaii in the central Pacific, lie far from plate edges. The magma here comes from a 'hot spot' in the mantle, where magma is probably created by radioactive heat.

Some volcanoes are explosive. When they erupt, they explode clouds of hot ash and gases into the air. Other volcanoes are quiet. There are no massive explosions when they erupt. Instead, runny lava gushes out of the volcano's *vent* (opening) and builds up low, *shield* volcanoes. Most volcanoes are intermediate in type, sometimes erupting explosively and sometimes quietly. Intermediate volcanoes have *composite* cones, composed of alternating layers of hardened lava and compacted ash.

Scientific stations have been built around active volcanoes in thickly populated areas, such as at

Mount Vesuvius in Italy. Any changes in heat and pressure inside the volcano are carefully watched. And instruments called *tiltometers* measure any changes in the gradient of the sides of a volcano caused by the swelling of magma below. The scientists issue warnings when they think an eruption is likely.

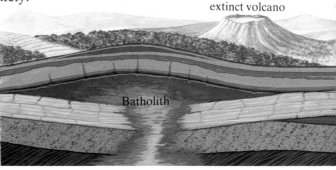

Lake in extinct volcano

Batholith

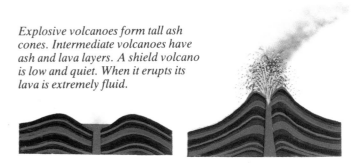

Explosive volcanoes form tall ash cones. Intermediate volcanoes have ash and lava layers. A shield volcano is low and quiet. When it erupts its lava is extremely fluid.

Mountain Building

The three main kinds of mountains are volcanoes, fold mountains and block mountains.

Fold mountains are formed by enormous lateral (sideways) pressure. This pressure twists and buckles formerly flat rock layers into loops, called *folds*. A simple upfold is called an *anticline*, and a downfold is a *syncline*. An *anticlinorium* is a large anticline, containing within it many small anticlines. Sometimes, folds are turned on their sides. These are called *recumbent* folds. Sometimes, folds are broken away and pushed many kilometres over other rocks; such folds are called *nappes*.

How then did the world's highest fold mountains, the Himalayas in northern India, form? About 200 million years ago, the Indian land mass was joined to Africa and Antarctica.

Around 180 million years ago, this plate began to

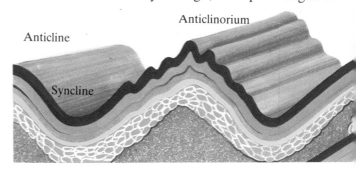

Anticlinorium

Anticline

Syncline

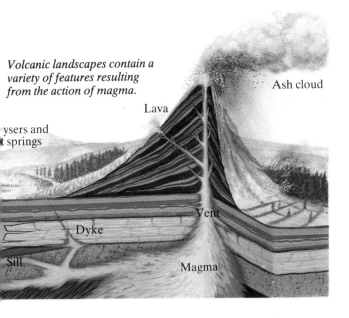

Volcanic landscapes contain a variety of features resulting from the action of magma.

Ash cloud

Lava

ysers and springs

Vent

Dyke

Sill

Magma

Limestone caves are worn out by chemical weathering. They are dissolved by rainwater which has dissolved carbon dioxide from the air and the soil, so becoming a weak acid.

drift away. By about 50 million years ago, it was pushing against the huge Asian plate. The rocks on the sea bed between the two plates were squeezed together. They slowly rose up to form the Himalayan range. Today, the Indian and Asian plates are firmly joined together. The lofty Himalayas are mostly formed from sedimentary rocks that piled up in a sea that no longer exists. Fossils of sea creatures have been found near the top of Mount Everest, the highest peak in the Himalayas.

Other fold mountains include the Alps in Europe. They began to rise about 26 million years ago when a plate bearing Italy pushed against the European plate. Other major fold mountains include the Andes in South America and the Rockies in North America.

Block mountains, or *horsts*, are blocks of land that were squeezed up between long faults in the Earth's crust. Blocks of land also sank between faults to form steep-sided rift valleys, or *graben*. Like fold mountains, these features are caused by plate movements. Examples of block mountains include the Ruwenzori range which overlooks the deep East African Rift Valley. In Europe, the Vosges Mountains and the Black Forest are block mountains bordering a rift valley that contains the River Rhine.

Great sideways pressure squeezes rocks into anticlines, synclines, complex anticlinoriums and nappes. Fold mountains are formed when two plates are pushed against each other. Block mountains and rift valleys form between parallel sets of faults.

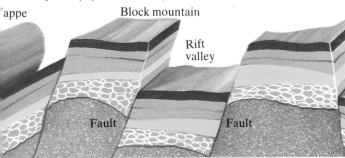

appe

Block mountain

Rift valley

Fault

Fault

Weathering

Even as mountain ranges are being formed, natural forces wear them down. Natural erosion continues all the time. On average, a depth of about 3.5 cm of land is stripped off all land surfaces every 1000 years.

One group of natural forces is called weathering. Mechanical weathering includes frost action, which occurs because ice takes up over nine per cent more space than the water from which it was formed. Hence, when water freezes in the cracks in rocks the ice exerts pressure. It widens the cracks until bits of rock break away. In mountain areas, the rock fragments pile up in huge heaps called scree or talus. In hot deserts, intense heating and rapid cooling make the outer layers of rocks peel away. Mechanical weathering also includes the action of plants and burrowing animals, which break up rocks.

Rocks shattered by frost action in rainy mountain areas pile up in heaps called scree.

Rivers

Rivers are important in eroding the land. The Mississippi River alone sweeps more than 700 million tonnes of sediment into the sea every year.

Rivers rise in springs, lakes or in melting glaciers. Youthful rivers usually have a small volume, but when they are swollen by heavy rain or melting snow, they become torrents. They sweep loose rocks downstream and this material wears out more rocks from the river bed. In this way, youthful rivers carve out deep V-shaped valleys. When they reach gentler slopes, the rivers enter maturity. They occupy broader valleys, and often contain sweeping curves called *meanders*. Tributary rivers increase their volume so that they can carry a large load of sediment, while still wearing out their valleys.

In old age, the volume of water is great, but the rivers are sluggish as they cross nearly flat plains. Muddy from their load, they often flood and spread sediment over the plains. The largest particles are dropped first on the river banks, building up mounds called *levees*. Old age rivers may change course and former meanders become swampy *oxbow lakes*.

The rivers finally discharge into the sea. If there are no strong offshore currents, the sediment may accumulate in new land areas called *deltas*. Otherwise, it is swept out to sea where it piles up on the sea bed to form sedimentary rocks.

The Work of Ice

About two per cent of the world's water is locked in ice sheets, ice caps and valley glaciers. Moving ice can cut deeply into the land. Rocks frozen in the bottom and sides of the ice give it the power of a giant file. Glaciers form in mountain basins from compacted snow. The ice spills out of the basins and flows downhill along valleys. Most glaciers flow only about one metre a day. But the speed increases if heavy snowfall or avalanches pile up snow on the glacier's source. Glaciers carry huge loads of frost-shattered rocks called *moraine*. This is either on the surface or frozen in the ice.

Ice wears out distinctive features. Much glaciated scenery exists in the northern hemisphere in areas now free from ice. This land was under the grip of an Ice Age only 10,000 to 20,000 years ago.

In mountains, the basins, or *cirques*, in which glaciers form, are steep-sided. They often contain small lakes called *tarns* after the ice has gone. Cirques are separated from each other by knife-edged ridges called *arêtes*. And if three or more cirques are back to back, the ice carves out a pointed peak, called a *horn*. The most obvious features of all are steep-sided, U-shaped valleys, quite unlike the V-shaped river valleys. Other glacial features are formed from moraine. This eroded material, ranging from boulders to clay, forms low hills, winding ridges and clusters of hummocks.

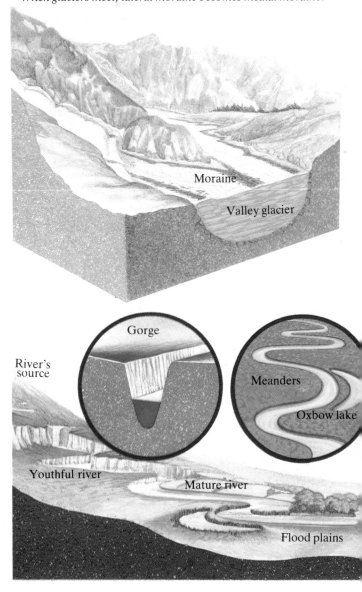

Valley glaciers in mountain regions transport moraine (loose rock). Moraine on the glacier's sides is called lateral moraine. When glaciers meet, lateral moraine becomes medial moraine.

Moraine

Valley glacier

Gorge

River's source

Meanders

Oxbow lake

Youthful river

Mature river

Flood plains

The Work of the Wind

Hot deserts occur in all continents except Europe. Although the average rainfall is low, much desert scenery has been shaped by running water. This may have occurred in the past when the climate was much wetter than it is today. Or it may be caused by occasional storms. The rain may be so intense that large areas are flooded and torrents wear out gullies called *wadis*. Finally, the water sinks into the ground or is evaporated by the Sun.

Normally, the wind is the chief agent of erosion in deserts. Winds carry dust high into the air and lift sand grains a metre or so above the ground. Wind-blown sand moves by bouncing on the surface. As it moves, it polishes and undercuts rocks, scours the ground to create hollows, strips the paint off cars, and cuts right through wooden telegraph poles.

Vast seas of sand, called by an Arabic word *erg*, cover about one-fifth of the hot deserts.

Coasts

While weathering, rivers and ice mould the scenery of inland areas, the sea is the great sculptor of coasts. Waves pound the shore and, in severe storms, they have moved blocks of concrete of 1000 tonnes or more. In storms, waves are armed with stones which they lift up and hurl at cliffs. This bombardment wears out caves at the base of cliffs. Finally, the overlying rocks are dislodged and crash down. Waves also trap and compress air in cracks and holes in rocks. When the pressure is released, the air expands explosively, enlarging cracks or shattering the rocks. The sea dissolves some rocks. It also churns loose rocks together until they become smooth pebbles. Many years of continual churning reduces the pebbles to sand.

Waves erode soft rocks to create bays. Headlands between bays are made up of harder rocks which have

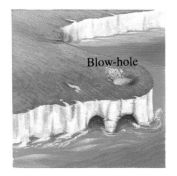
Blow-hole

Stack

New caves

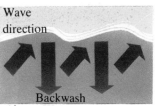
Wave direction

Backwash

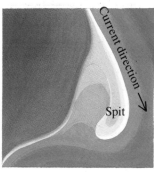
Current direction

Spit

Above: Waves transport material along beaches by longshore drift. Right: The material may be dumped in long spits.

Youthful rivers flow swiftly through deep valleys in their upper courses. Mature rivers develop large meanders and some old age rivers are enclosed by levees. Deltas may form at the river mouth.

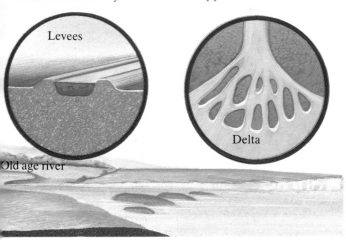
Levees

Delta

Old age river

When mountains are freed of snow and ice, such features as pyramidal peaks, knife-edged ridges, cirques and deep, U-shaped valleys testify to glaciation in the past.

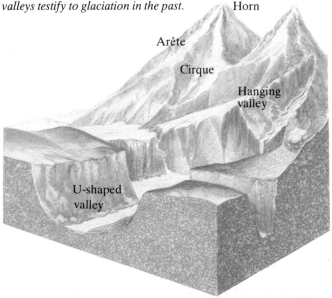
Horn

Arête

Cirque

Hanging valley

U-shaped valley

resisted erosion. But even headlands are eventually worn back, as shown in the diagrams at the bottom of this page. Coasts most vulnerable to wave erosion are those made up of loose deposits, such as moraine deposited by glaciers.

Waves and currents transport loose rocks and sand along beaches in a process called *longshore drift*. This is a zig-zag movement which occurs because waves usually sweep diagonally up a beach, pushing loose material along with them. But the backwash always carries the material down at right angles to the beach. Worn material may be swept out to sea, but waves also build new land areas.

Man's Home

About 10,000 years ago, about 8 million people lived on Earth. In the mid-1970s, the world's population passed the 4000 million mark and, by the year 2000, it will probably reach 6000 million. The rapid growth of population is putting a strain on the Earth's resources. For example, increasing amounts of food have been needed, but poor farming methods and overgrazing have caused severe soil erosion. Much farmland has been made infertile and much rich soil has been lost. Nature renews the soil lost by natural erosion. But when the soil is damaged by man-induced soil erosion, it takes a long time before Nature can replace it. There is also a mounting pressure on other resources. Known reserves of oil are likely to run dry in 20 to 30 years time and there may be shortages of many metals.

The factories that produce goods for the world's increasing population have been making Earth a less pleasant place on which to live. Land, sea and air have been polluted by industrial wastes. We are now faced with the challenge of conserving and protecting the Earth's many gifts for unborn generations.

MAPS

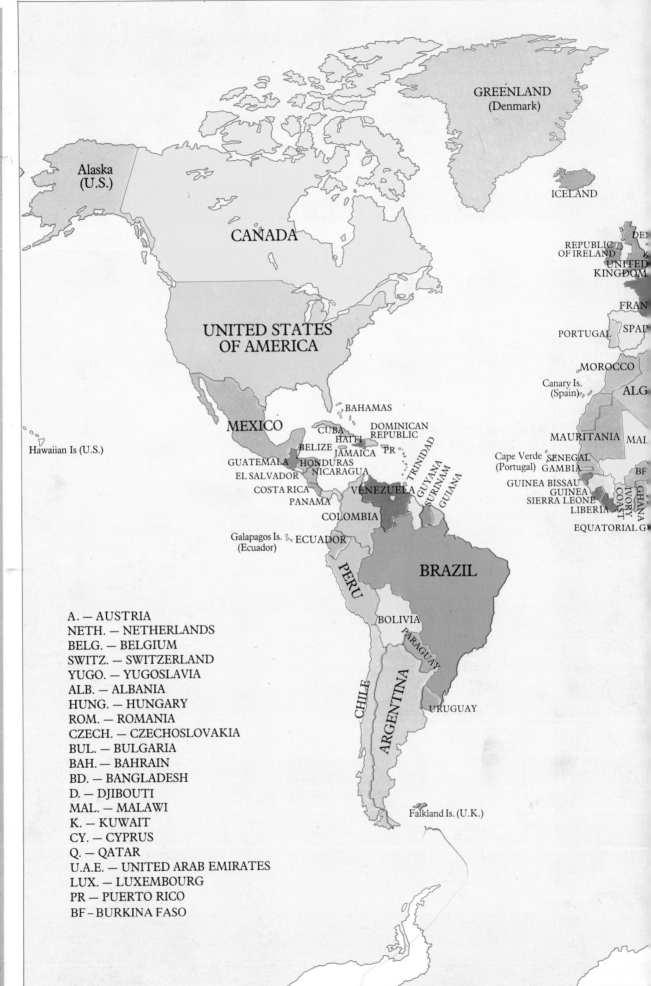

GREENLAND
(Denmark)

ICELAND

Alaska
(U.S.)

CANADA

REPUBLIC
OF IRELAND
UNITED
KINGDOM

FRAN

PORTUGAL   SPAI

UNITED STATES
OF AMERICA

MOROCCO

Canary Is.
(Spain)   ALG

BAHAMAS

MEXICO

CUBA   DOMINICAN
HAITI   REPUBLIC
BELIZE   JAMAICA   PR

MAURITANIA   MAL

Hawaiian Is (U.S.)

GUATEMALA   HONDURAS
EL SALVADOR   NICARAGUA

Cape Verde   SENEGAL
(Portugal)   GAMBIA   BF

GUINEA BISSAU
GUINEA
SIERRA LEONE   IVORY COAST   GHANA
LIBERIA

COSTA RICA
PANAMA

VENEZUELA

TRINIDAD
GUYANA
SURINAM
GUIANA

COLOMBIA

EQUATORIAL G

Galapagos Is.
(Ecuador)   ECUADOR

BRAZIL

PERU

BOLIVIA

A. — AUSTRIA
NETH. — NETHERLANDS
BELG. — BELGIUM
SWITZ. — SWITZERLAND
YUGO. — YUGOSLAVIA
ALB. — ALBANIA
HUNG. — HUNGARY
ROM. — ROMANIA
CZECH. — CZECHOSLOVAKIA
BUL. — BULGARIA
BAH. — BAHRAIN
BD. — BANGLADESH
D. — DJIBOUTI
MAL. — MALAWI
K. — KUWAIT
CY. — CYPRUS
Q. — QATAR
U.A.E. — UNITED ARAB EMIRATES
LUX. — LUXEMBOURG
PR — PUERTO RICO
BF – BURKINA FASO

PARAGUAY

CHILE

ARGENTINA

URUGUAY

Falkland Is. (U.K.)

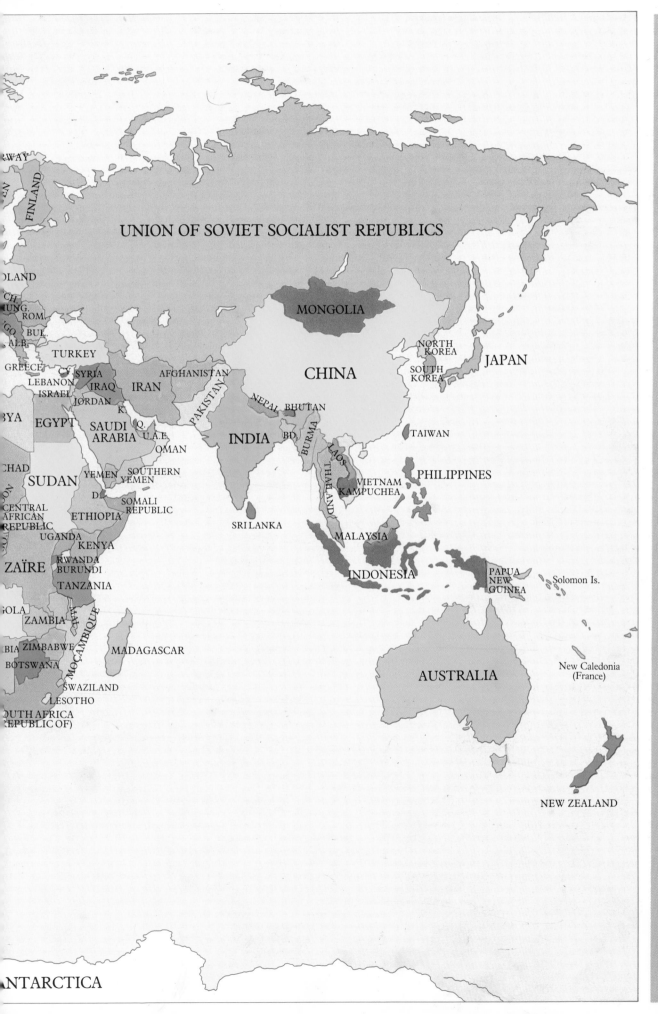

RWAY

FINLAND

UNION OF SOVIET SOCIALIST REPUBLICS

OLAND

CH.
UNG.
ROM.
GO.
ALB.
BUL.

TURKEY

GREECE

LEBANON
ISRAEL

CY.
SYRIA
IRAQ
JORDAN
K.

AFGHANISTAN

IRAN

PAKISTAN

BYA

EGYPT

SAUDI
ARABIA

Q.
U.A.E.

OMAN

CHAD

SUDAN

YEMEN
SOUTHERN
YEMEN

D.

SOMALI
REPUBLIC

CENTRAL
AFRICAN
REPUBLIC

ETHIOPIA

UGANDA

ZAÏRE

RWANDA
BURUNDI

KENYA

TANZANIA

GOLA

ZAMBIA

MOZAMBIQUE

BIA
ZIMBABWE

BOTSWANA

SWAZILAND

LESOTHO

OUTH AFRICA
EPUBLIC OF)

MONGOLIA

CHINA

NEPAL
BHUTAN

INDIA

BD.
BURMA

LAOS

THAILAND

SRI LANKA

NORTH
KOREA

SOUTH
KOREA

JAPAN

TAIWAN

VIETNAM
KAMPUCHEA

PHILIPPINES

MALAYSIA

INDONESIA

PAPUA
NEW
GUINEA

Solomon Is.

New Caledonia
(France)

MADAGASCAR

AUSTRALIA

NEW ZEALAND

NTARCTICA

A   B   C   D   ARCTIC   E

65°

ICELAND

Arctic Circle

30°

N O R W E G I A N   S E A

S C A N D I N A V I A

55°

Galdhöpiggen
2469

NORWAY

Lake
Vänern

ATLANTIC

▲ Ben Nevis
1343

SWEDEN

N O R T H
S E A

20°

OCEAN

IRELAND

UNITED
KINGDOM

DENMARK

BALTIC
SEA

POLAND

NETHERLANDS

North

Thames

WEST   EAST
GERMANY

English Channel

BELGIUM

Rhine

Elbe

Oder

Vistu

Seine

LUXEMBOURG

45°

Danube

CZECHOSLOVAKI

Bay of

Loire

LIECHTENSTEIN

Biscay

FRANCE

SWITZERLAND

AUSTRIA

Hunga

Garonne

MASSIF

A   L   P   S

HUNG

CANTABRIAN
MTS

Rhône

▲ Mt Blanc
4807

Po

CENTRAL

Duero

PYRÉNÉES

ANDORRA

MONACO

ITALY

SAN MARINO

Sava

DINARIC ALPS

PORTUGAL

Ebro

▲ Pico de Aneto
3404

LIGURIAN
SEA

M
e
s
e
t
a

ADRIATIC

YUGOSLA

Tagus

SPAIN

A
P
E
N
N
I
N
E
S

SEA

Guadiana

ALBA

Guadalquivir

SIERRA
NEVADA

TYRRHENIAN
SEA

35°

Str. of Gibraltar

M E D I T E R R A N E A N

IONIA

▲ Mt Etna
3340

SEA

TELL ATLAS

S E A

MOROCCO

ALGERIA

TUNISIA

MALTA

10°

20

0°   10°

F   G   OCEAN   H   J   1   K   2

70°

Pechora

Narodynaya
1894

U R A L   M T S

Ob

West
Siberian
Plain

White Sea

N. Dvina

FINLAND

Lake
Onega

Lake
Ladoga

Gulf of Finland

Kama

Volga

U   S   S   R   3

60°

W. Dvina

Ural

Central Russian

ropean

Plain

Kirghiz
Steppe

Uplands

Dnestr

Dnieper

Donets

Don

Volga

Ust Urt
Plateau

RPATHIANS

Sea of Azov

C A S P I A N   S E A

ROMANIA

B L A C K   S E A

Elbrus
5633m

CAUCASUS   MTS

4

BULGARIA

ALKAN MTS

PONTINE

Kizil   R A N G E

Mt Ararat
5165

ELBURZ MTS

npus
11

TURKEY

AEGEAN
SEA

GREECE

TAURUS MTS

Euphrates

Tigris

IRAN

CYPRUS

SYRIA

IRAQ   5

30°   40°   50°

21

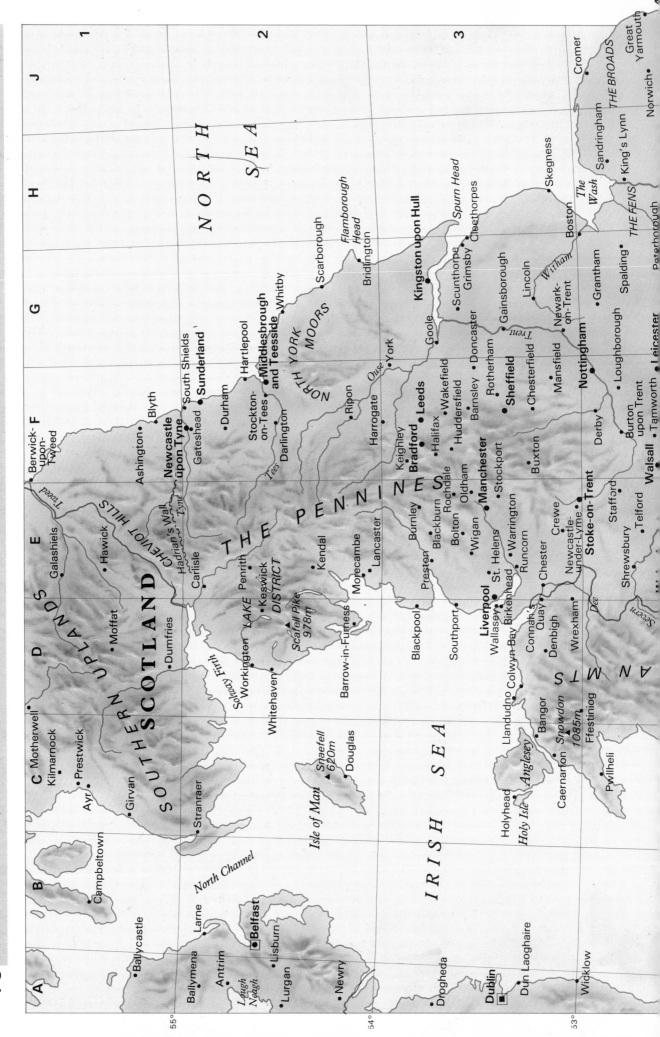

NORTH SEA

IRISH SEA

North Channel

Solway Firth

THE PENNINES

LAKE DISTRICT

NORTH YORK MOORS

SOUTHERN UPLANDS

SCOTLAND

CHEVIOT HILLS

Hadrian's Wall

CAMBRIAN MTS

THE FENS

THE BROADS

The Wash

Isle of Man

Anglesey

Holy Isle

Scafell Pike 978m

Snaefell 620m

Snowdon 1085m

Flamborough Head

Spurn Head

Ballycastle
Ballymena
Antrim
Lough Neagh
Larne
Lurgan
Newry
Lisburn
Belfast
Drogheda
Dublin
Dun Laoghaire
Wicklow

Campbeltown
Motherwell **C**
Kilmarnock
Prestwick
Ayr
Girvan
Stranraer
B

Galashiels
Hawick
Moffat
Dumfries
E
Berwick-upon-Tweed **F**

Carlisle
Workington
Whitehaven
Keswick
Penrith
Kendal
Barrow-in-Furness
Morecambe
Lancaster

Ashington
Blyth
South Shields
Newcastle upon Tyne
Gateshead
Sunderland
Durham
Hartlepool
Stockton-on-Tees
Middlesbrough and Teesside
Darlington
Whitby
Scarborough
Bridlington

Douglas

Holyhead
Llandudno
Colwyn Bay
Bangor
Caernarfon
Pwllheli
Ffestiniog
Denbigh
Connah's Quay
Wrexham

Blackpool
Southport
Preston
Burnley
Blackburn
Rochdale
Bolton
Oldham
Wigan
Liverpool
Wallasey
Birkenhead
St. Helens
Runcorn
Warrington
Manchester
Stockport
Crewe
Chester
Newcastle-under-Lyme
Stoke-on-Trent
Shrewsbury
Telford
Stafford

Ripon
Harrogate
York
Keighley
Bradford **Leeds**
Halifax
Huddersfield
Wakefield
Barnsley
Doncaster
Rotherham
Sheffield
Chesterfield
Buxton
Mansfield
Derby
Burton upon Trent
Tamworth
Walsall

Goole
Kingston upon Hull
Scunthorpe
Grimsby
Cleethorpes
Gainsborough
Lincoln
Newark-on-Trent
Nottingham
Loughborough
Leicester

Skegness
Boston
Spalding
Grantham
Peterborough

Cromer
Great Yarmouth
Norwich
Sandringham
King's Lynn

Tweed
Tyne
Tees
Ouse
Trent
Witham
Dee
Severn

J 1 2 3
H
G
F
E
D
C
B
A

55°
54°
53°

St. George's Channel

WALES

ENGLAND

FRANCE

Bury St. Edmunds
Ipswich
Felixstowe
Harwich
Colchester
Cambridge
Chelmsford
Basildon
Southend
Grays
Gravesend
Margate
Ramsgate
Canterbury
Dover
Folkestone
Ashford
Maidstone
Hastings
Eastbourne

5
6
7

Strait of Dover

Dieppe
Rouen
Seine
Fécamp
Le Havre
Caen
Cherbourg

Wellingborough
Northampton
Bedford
Luton
Harlow
St. Albans
Watford
London
Croydon
Gillingham
Slough
High Wycombe
Windsor
Reading
Milton Keynes
CHILTERN HILLS
Oxford
Stratford-upon-Avon
Worcester
Avon
Cheltenham
Gloucester
Stroud
Pontypool
Newport
COTSWOLDS
Thames
Swindon
Basingstoke
Woking
Guildford
Horsham
NORTH DOWNS
SOUTH DOWNS
Winchester
Tunbridge Wells
Brighton
Worthing
Chichester
Bognor Regis
Southampton
Havant
Portsmouth
Ryde
Newport
Isle of Wight

Hereford
Wye
Llandrindod Wells
Severn
Bristol
Bath
Cardiff
Weston-super-Mare
Barry
Bridgwater
Stonehenge
Salisbury
Wyle
Avon
Bournemouth
Poole
Weymouth
Dorchester
Yeovil

Brecon
BRECON BEACONS
Merthyr Tydfil
Aberdare
Rhondda
Pontypridd
Port Talbot
Swansea
Llanelli
Carmarthen
Cardigan
Fishguard
Milford Haven
Pembroke
Teifi

EXMOOR
Taunton
Ilfracombe
Barnstaple
Bideford
Okehampton
Exeter
Torbay
DARTMOOR
Plymouth
Tamar
BODMIN MOOR
St Austell
Truro
Falmouth
Newquay
Penzance
Land's End
Lizard Point
Is. of Scilly

Bristol Channel

ENGLISH CHANNEL

Alderney
Guernsey
St. Peter Port
Sark
Jersey
St. Helier
Channel Islands

0°
1°
2°
3°
4°
5°

52°
51°
50°

miles
0   20   40   60
0   20 40 60 80 100
kilometres

23

SCOTLAND

Shetland Islands

Lerwick

at same scale

A B C D E F G

miles

0   20   40   60

0   20   40   60   80   100
kilometres

Fair Isle

ATLANTIC OCEAN

Orkney Islands

Kirkwall

1

59°

60°

1°

Pentland Firth

John O'Groats

Thurso

Wick

2

NORTH SEA

Loch Shin

Helmsdale

Lairg

OUTER HEBRIDES

Stornoway

Lewis

Tarbert

Harris

Ullapool

Moray Firth

Banff

Fraserburgh

Cromarty

Elgin

Keith

Peterhead

NORTH WEST HIGHLANDS

Dingwall

Nairn

Huntly

3

North Uist

Portree

Stromeferry

Inverness

Grantown-on-Spey

Skye

Kyle of Lochalsh

Loch Ness

Spey

Don

Aberdeen

South Uist

Broadford

GLEN MORE

Dee

Eriskay

CAIRNGORMS

Ben Macdhui
1311m

Ballater

57°

Barra

Rhum

Braemar

Stonehaven

Eigg

Fort William
Ben Nevis
1343m

GRAMPIAN MOUNTAINS

Brechin

Montrose

Coll

Pitlochry

Forfar

INNER HEBRIDES

Tiree

Tay

Arbroath

4

Mull

Oban

Loch Tay

Dundee

Firth of Lorn

Perth

SCOTLAND

St. Andrews

Firth of Tay

Callander

Glenrothes

Jura

Loch Lomond

Stirling

Kirkcaldy

56°

Dunfermline

Firth of Forth

Dunbar

Dumbarton

Greenock

Clydebank

Cumbernauld

Falkirk

Edinburgh

Islay

Paisley

Glasgow

Coatbridge

Hamilton

Motherwell

Wishaw

Berwick-upon-Tweed

Peebles

East Kilbride

Clyde

Galashiels

Tweed

Arran

Irvine

Kilmarnock

SOUTHERN UPLANDS

North Channel

Campbeltown

Firth of Clyde

Ayr

Prestwick

5

Portrush

Girvan

Moffat

Hawick

Coleraine

NORTHERN IRELAND

Londonderry

Ballymena

Larne

Stranraer

Newton Stewart

Dumfries

ENGLAND

Carlisle

Solway Firth

6

55°

7°   6°   5°   4°   3°   2°

24

miles
0   20   40   60
kilometres
0   20   40   60   80   100

A   B   C   D   E   F

1

North Channel

Portrush
Buncrana   Coleraine   Ballycastle
Lough
Foyle
Londonderry
Larne
Strabane   *Bann*   Ballymena
NORTHERN
IRELAND   Antrim   *Belfast Lough*
Newtownabbey   Bangor
Donegal   Omagh   *Lough*   ☒**Belfast**
Ballyshannon   *Neagh*   Lisburn   2
Donegal Bay   *Lower*   Portadown   Lurgan
Lough Erne
Enniskillen   Armagh   Downpatrick
Sligo
Upper   Monaghan   Newry
Lough Erne

Carrickmacross   Dundalk
Ballina   Carrick-on-Shannon
Lough   *IRISH*
Conn   *SEA*
Achill
Isle   Castlebar   Longford   Kells
Westport   Drogheda   3
Lough   Roscommon
Mask   **REPUBLIC OF IRELAND**
Lough   *Lough Ree*
Clifden   *Corrib*   Athlone   **Dublin** Howth
Athenry   Clara   *Liffey*   ☒
Galway   Ballinasloe   Naas   Dun Laoghaire
Galway Bay   *Shannon*   Kildare
Port Laoise
Aran Is   Athy   Wicklow
Lough Derg   Roscrea   Carlow
Ennis   Nenagh   *Barrow*   Arklow
Kilkee   Thurles
Kilrush   Kilkenny   4
Limerick   Cashel   New Ross   Wexford
Tipperary
Clonmel   Waterford
Tralee   *Blackwater*   Dungarvan
Dingle   Killarney   Mallow
Dingle Bay   Youghal
▲Carrantuohill   Cork
1041m   Kenmare   Cobh
Bandon
Bantry
Bantry Bay   5

ATLANTIC OCEAN

St. George's Channel

WICKLOW MTS

5°
4°
3°
2°
0°

10°   9°   8°   7°   6°

25

A   B   C   D   E

ENGLAND

Southampton
Brighton
Exeter   Bournemouth   Portsmouth
Dove
Plymouth   Isle of Wight
Torbay
50°
Penzance   Truro

English Channel

Alderney

Dieppe

Guernsey   Cherbourg   Le Havre
Sark   Ro
Channel Islands
Br.   *Jersey*
St. Helier   Caen

Île d'Ouessant   Alençon

Brest   • Morlaix   St. Malo
48°   St. Brieuc   • Fougères

Quimper   Rennes

Le Mans
Lorient

• Vannes   **F   R**

Belle Île   *Loire*   • Angers   Tours
St. Nazaire
Nantes   • Cholet
Île de Noirmoutier   Châtellerault

Île d'Yeu   • La Roche-
sur-Yon   Poitiers

46°   *Île de Ré*

Île d'Oléron
Cognac   Limog
Bay   of   Angoulême

Gironde
Biscay   Périgue

miles   Bergerac
0   50   100   Bordeaux   *Dordogne*
0   50   100   150
kilometres

44°   Lo

• Agen

Montau
Gulf of Gascony
Dax   *Adour*
• Gijón   Santander   **Toulo**
Biarritz   Bayonne
Oviedo   Torrelavega   **Bilbao**
San Sebastián   Pau
SPAIN   • Tarbes
• Vitoria   • Lourdes
P Y R É N É E S
• Pamplona   *Pic de*
Vignemale ▲   *Pico de Aneto*
3298   3404 ▲

6°   4°   2°   0°

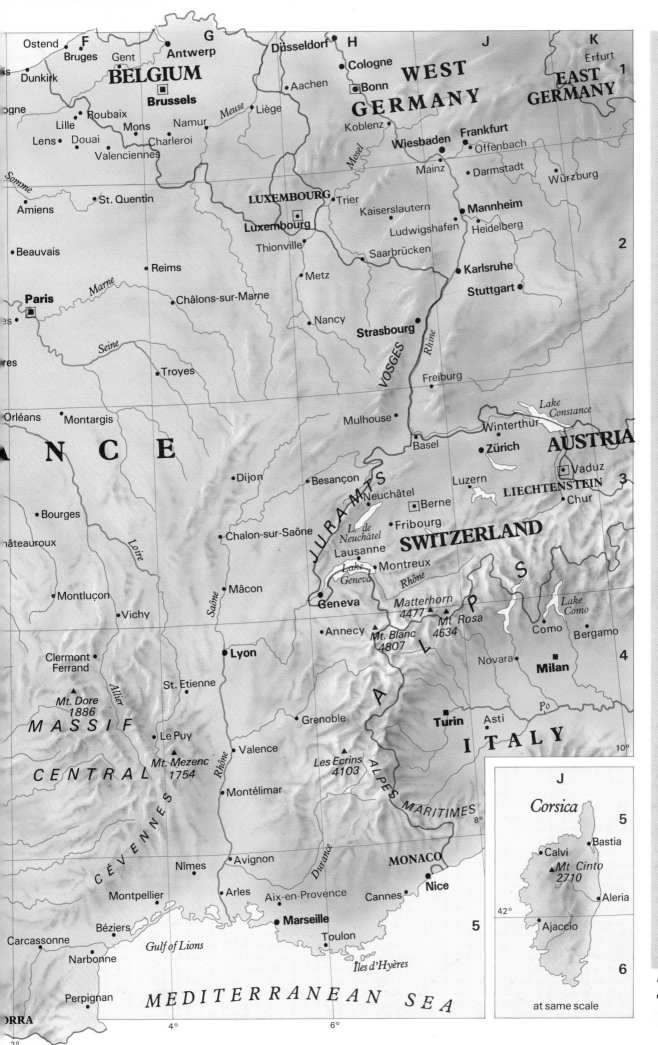

Ostend • F • G • Düsseldorf • H • J • K • Erfurt

Dunkirk • Bruges • Gent • Antwerp • Cologne • WEST • EAST
...ogne • BELGIUM • Aachen • Bonn • GERMANY • GERMANY

Lille • Roubaix • Mons • Brussels • Liège • Koblenz
Lens • Douai • Charleroi • Namur • Meuse • Frankfurt
Valenciennes • Wiesbaden • Offenbach

Somme • Mainz • Darmstadt • Würzburg

Amiens • St. Quentin • LUXEMBOURG • Trier • Mannheim
Beauvais • Luxembourg • Kaiserslautern • Heidelberg
Thionville • Ludwigshafen • Saarbrücken • Karlsruhe

Reims • Metz • Stuttgart
Paris • Marne • Châlons-sur-Marne • Nancy • Strasbourg

Seine • Troyes • VOSGES • Rhine • Freiburg

Orléans • Montargis • Lake Constance
ANCE • Mulhouse • Winterthur • AUSTRIA
Basel • Zürich • Vaduz

Dijon • Besançon • Luzern • LIECHTENSTEIN • Chur
Bourges • JURA MTS • Neuchâtel • Berne
...âteauroux • L. de Neuchâtel • Fribourg • SWITZERLAND
Chalon-sur-Saône • Lausanne
Lake Geneva • Montreux • Rhône • Lake Como
Montluçon • Mâcon • Geneva • Matterhorn 4477 • Mt Rosa 4634 • Como • Bergamo
Vichy • Annecy • Mt. Blanc 4807 • Novara • Milan

Clermont Ferrand • Lyon
Mt. Dore 1886 • St. Etienne
MASSIF • Le Puy • Grenoble • Turin • Asti • ITALY • Po
CENTRAL • Mt. Mezenc 1754 • Valence • Les Ecrins 4103 • ALPES MARITIMES
Montélimar

CÉVENNES • Nîmes • Avignon • MONACO
Montpellier • Arles • Aix-en-Provence • Cannes • Nice
Béziers • Marseille
Carcassonne • Gulf of Lions • Toulon
Narbonne • Îles d'Hyères
Perpignan • MEDITERRANEAN SEA
...ORRA

Corsica
Bastia
Calvi • Mt Cinto 2710
Ajaccio • Aleria
at same scale

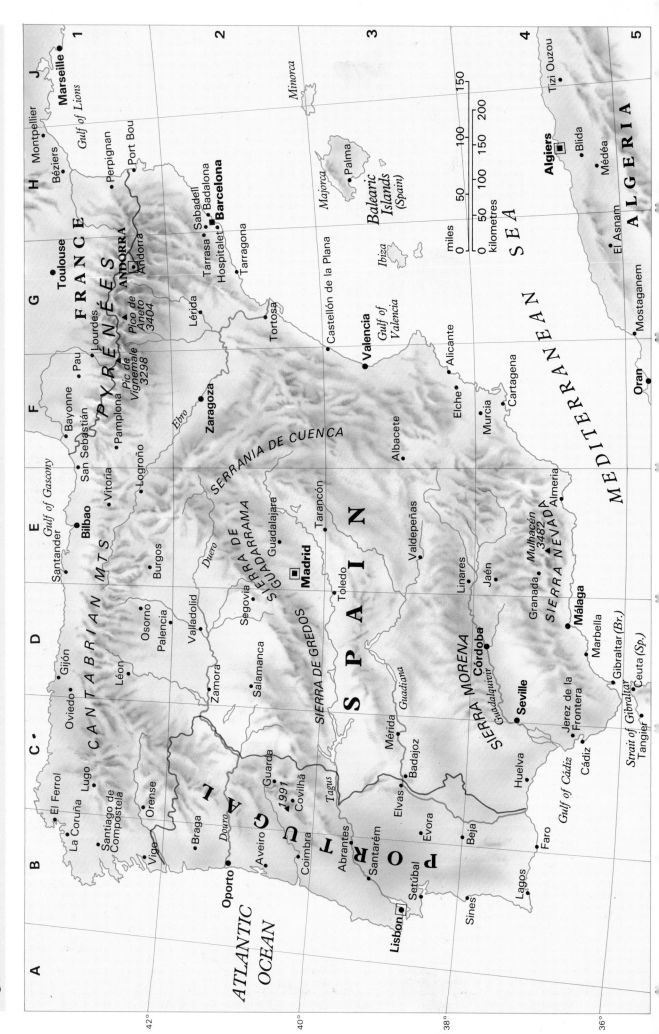

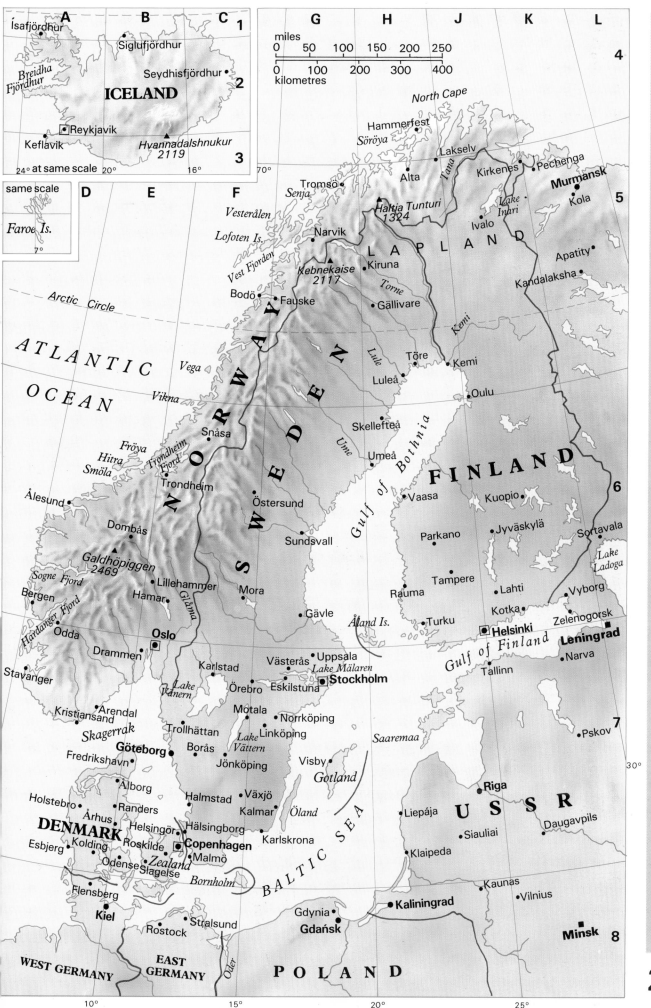

miles
0   50   100
0   50   100   150
kilometres

54°

NORTH SEA

DENMARK
Flensburg
Kiel
Neumünster
Stralsund
Rostock
Greifs
Lübeck
Wismar
Schwerin
Neubrander

East Frisian Is.
West Frisian Is.
Wadden Sea
Bremerhaven
Hamburg

EAST

Groningen
Assen
Wilhelmshaven
Oldenburg
Bremen
Wittenberge

NETHERLANDS
WEST
Haarlem
Zwolle
Amsterdam
Osnabrück
Hanover
Wolfsburg
Potsdam

52°
The Hague
Apeldoorn
Enschede
Utrecht
Ems
Weser
Brunswick
Salzgitter
GERMA
Rotterdam
Arnhem
Münster
Bielefeld
Magdeburg
Dordrecht
Maas
HARZ MTS
Elbe
Dessau

Eindhoven
Duisburg
Gelsenkirchen
GERMANY
Halle
Lauchha
Antwerp
Essen
Dortmund
Bochum
Kassel
Leipzig
Meisse
Brussels
Mönchen-Gladbach
Wuppertal
Düsseldorf
Weimar
Dre
Maastricht
Cologne
Erfurt
Gera
BELGIUM
Aachen
Bonn
Siegen
Thuringian Forest
Karl Marx Stadt
Charleroi
Rhine
Wetzlar
Fulda
Zwickau

50°
ARDENNES
EIFEL
Koblenz
ORE M
Karlovy

Mosel
Wiesbaden
Frankfurt
Offenbach
Bayreuth
Charleville-Mézières
LUXEMBOURG
Mainz
Main
Bamberg
Plze
Luxembourg
Kaiserslautern
Darmstadt
Würzburg
Bohemian Forest
Thionville
Mannheim
Fürth
Verdun
Saarbrücken
Heidelberg
Nuremberg
Metz
Karlsruhe
Regensburg
St. Dizier
Nancy
Stuttgart
Danube
Strasbourg
Rhine
VOSGES
Offenburg
Black Forest
Ulm
Augsburg

48°
FRANCE
Freiburg
Munich
Mulhouse
Memmingen
Inn
Lake Constance
Kempten
Dijon
Doubs
Basel
Zugspitze 2963
Sa
Besançon
Winterthur
Zürich
JURA MTS
Luzern
Lake Zürich
LIECHTENSTEIN
Innsbruck
Saône
Berne
Vaduz
Gross Glockr 3798
L. de Neuchâtel
SWITZERLAND
Chur
AU
Lausanne
ALPS
Merano
Geneva
Lake Geneva
Jungfrau 4158
ITALY
Bolzano

6°   8°   10°   12°

A   B   C   D   E

F G H J K

BALTIC SEA

Gulf of Gdańsk

Kaliningrad
Chernyakhovsk
U S S R
Kaunas

Gdynia
1

Gdańsk
Elbląg
Olsztyn
Grodno

Kołobrzeg
Koszalin
Malbork
2

Wolin
Chojnice

Szczecin
Stargard
Łomża
Białystok

Piła
Bydgoszcz
Toruń
Pułtusk

Inowrocław
Włocławek
Brest

Kostrzyn
Poznań
P O L A N D
Warsaw
Siedlce

ankfurt
Oder
Vistula

Gubin
Leszno
Kalisz
Łódź
Radom
Lublin
3

tbus
Neisse
Glogów

Spree
Legnica
Wrocław
Zamość

Görlitz

Liberec
Walbrzych
Czestochowa

ti nad Labem
S U D E T E N   M T S
Zabrze
Chorzów
Rzeszów

Katowice
Krakow
Tarnow

Prague
Krakow
Przemyśl

Ostrava
C A R P A T H I A N   M T S

CZECHOSLOVAKIA
Olomouc
Rysy 2499
4

Vltava
Jihlava
Gerlachovka Stit 2655

Brno
Váh
Košice
Uzhgorod

Trěbŏn
Znojmo
Mukachevo

Gmünd
Miskolc

Krems
Satu Mare

Linz
Bratislava

St. Polten
Vienna
Kékes 1015
Tisza

Lake Neusiedlen
Győr
Danube
Debrecen

Budapest

Leoben
Szombathely
H U N G A R Y
Oradea
5

RIA
Lake Balaton

Graz
Kecskemet

agenfurt
Maribor
Nagykanizsa
Szeged
Arad
ROMANIA

Pécs

16° 20° 22°

A B C D E F

SWITZERLAND
Berne Luzern
LIECHTENSTEIN
Vaduz
Landeck
Innsbruck
Kufstein
Kapfenberg
Gyö
AUSTRIA
Leoben
Szombathely
Graz
Lausanne
Interlaken
Montreux
Rhône
Jungfrau
4158
Davos
St. Moritz
Gross
Glockner
3798
Spittal
Lienz
Klagenfurt
Villach
DOLOMITES
Maribor
Lake
Balaton
Nagykan
Geneva
Matterhorn
4477
Locarno
Lake
Como
Adige
Udine
Ljubljana
Gorizia
Zagreb
Virovitica
Mont Blanc
4807
Mt Rosa
4634
Lake
Maggiore
Bergamo
Lake
Garda
Trieste
FRANCE
Novara
Monza
Brescia
Verona
Padua
Venice
Rijeka
Karlovac
Ogulin
Dubica
Sa
Vercelli
Milan
Turin
Mt Viso
3847
Alessandria
Po
Parma
Ferrara
Gulf of
Venice
Banja Luk
YUGO
Genoa
Modena
Bologna
Ravenna
DINARIC
La Spezia
A P E
Forli
Rimini
Zadar
Nice
Gulf of
Genoa
Florence
San Marino
ADRIATIC
ALPS
MONACO
Pisa
N
Lake
Trasimeno
Mt Vettore
2476
Ancona
Split
Mosta
LIGURIAN SEA
Livorno
Arno
Terni
N
Metković
Elba
Lake
Bolsena
Tiber
A
Mt Corno 2914
Pescara
SEA
Dubr
Calvi
Bastia
Mt Cinto
2710
Corte
Aléria
I
Mt Amaro
2794
Rome
Ajaccio
N
Corsica
(France)
Bonifacio
E
Foggia
Bari
Olbia
Sássari
Naples
Vesuvius
Y
Bosa
Macomer
Sardinia
(Italy)
Ischia
Salerno
Táranto
Oristano
Tirso
Arbatax
Capri
Villaputzu
TYRRHENIAN SEA
S
Cagliari
Cosenza
Lipari Is.
MEDITERRANEAN
Palermo
Messina
Roccella
Reggio
Trápani
Mt Etna
3340
Bizerte
Enna
Catania
Annaba
Tabarka
Mateur
Sicily
Vittória
Siracusa
ALGERIA
Tunis
Pantelleria
(Italy)
SEA
TUNISIA
Nabeul
Sousse
MALTA
Valletta
Mahdia

8° 10° 12° 14° 16°
36° 38° 40° 42° 44° 46°

G   H   J   K   L   M   N

□Budapest   Debrecen   Satu Mare   Botoşani   **Iaşi**   Kishinev   Tiraspol   1

Tisza   • Dej   **CARPATHIAN**   **Odessa ■**

Kecskemet   • Oradea   **Cluj**   • Bacâu   **MTS**

N G A R Y   *Danube*

Szeged   • Arad   • Tirgu Mureş   2

Subotica   Kikinda   **Timişoara**   • Alba Iulia   *Mures*

• Sombor   Lugoj   **TRANSYLVANIAN ALPS**   **Braşov**   **Galati**   • Izmail

• Zrenjanin   *Negoiu 2548*   Brăila   Tulcea

Novi Sad   **R O M A N I A**   Ploeşti   *Danube*   **Constanţa**

Belgrade □   Turnu Severin   • Piteşti   **□Bucharest**

A V I A   Craiova   • Mangalia   3

Kragujevac •   Caracal   Giurgiu •   Silistra   Tolbukhin •   Balchik

ajevo   • Vidin   • Ruse   • Razgrad

• Lom   **B**   **Varna**

Niš •   • Vratsa   • Pleven   **BLACK SEA**

• Nikšić   • Pec   Leskovac •   **B U L G A R I A**   Karnobat •   Burgas

• Titograd   • Priština   **LKAN MTS**   Stara   • Yambol

or   **Sofia**   Zagora

Bar   *Lake*   **Plovdiv**   Kirklareli •   • Midye   4

Shkodër   **Skopje**   Blagoevgrad   *Marisa*   • Luleburgaz   **Istanbul ■**

Shëngjin   • Shkodër   • Titov Veles   **RHODOPE MTS**   • Smolyan   Edirne   Tekirdağ   **SEA OF MARMARA**

Tiranë □   *Vardar*   Petrich   Komotini   Kesan   Bandirma

Durrës   *Ohridsko Lake*   • Kilkis   • Sérrai   Xánthi   Alexandroúpolis   **Bursa**

• Ohrid   Bitola   Gallipoli   Çanakkale

Elbasan   *Prespa Lake*   Edhessa   **Thessaloniki**   *Thásos*

ALBANIA   Korce •   • Kastoria   *Samothráki*   *Imroz*

Vlorë   **PINDUS**   *Mt Olympus 2911*   *Límnos*   **T U R K E Y**

of Oranto   Ioánnina   **Lárisa**   *Aegean*   Ayvalik   5

Corfu   Igoumenítsa   Trikkala   Vólos   Mitilíni   Bergama

MTS   Fársala   *Lésvos*   Manisa

Arta   Lamía   Skiros   Khíos   **Izmir**

Préveza   **G R E E C E**   *Euboea*

IONIAN   Mesolóngion   Návpaktos   Khalkis   Aydin

SEA   Marathon   Söke

Kefallinia   Pátrai   **□Athens**   Ándros   Samos   Milâs

Corinth   Piraeus   *Tínos*   6

Zákinthos   Pírgos   Argos •   *Kéa*   *Ikaría*   Marmaris

Návplion   *Kúthnos*   *Náxos*   *Kos*   Rhodes

Kalámai   *Milos*   *Rhodes*   Lindos

Pílos   *Thíra*

miles   *Kíthira*   **SEA OF CRETE**

50   100   150   7

50   100   150   200   *Kárpathos*

kilometres

Canea   *Crete*   Iráklion

20°   22°   24°   26°   28°   Réthimnon

33

60° 70° 80°

A B C D E

Arctic Circle

N O R W A Y

S W E D E N

FINLAND

A R C T I C

Franz Josef Land

Severn Zem

Novaya Zemlya

BARENTS SEA

KARA SEA

DENMARK
Oslo
Copenhagen
Stockholm

BALTIC SEA

Helsinki

Murmansk

Kolguyev

Vaygach

Tayr

White Sea

POLAND
Warsaw
Kaliningrad
Grodno
Brest
Lvov
Vilnius
Minsk
Gomel
Bryansk
Tallinn
Novgorod
Pskov
Riga
Vitebsk
Kalinin
Yaroslavl
Leningrad
Cherepovets
Lake Ladoga
Petrozavodsk
Lake Onega
Vologda
Arkhangel'sk
Dvina
Syktyvkar
Narodnaya 1894
Salekhard

West Siberian Plain

Dnieper
Kiev
Vinnitsa
Rovno
Kishinev
Dnepropetrovsk
Zaporozhye
Odessa
KrivoyRog
Kherson
Zhdanov
Simferopol'
Krasnodar
Sea of Azov
Sumy
Orel
Kursk
Tula
Ryazan
Moscow
Kostroma
Kirov
Gorki
Cheboksary
Izhevsk
Perm
Berezniki
Serov
U N I O N   O F   S O V I E

Kharkov
Voronezh
Donetsk
Rostov
Taganrog
Tambov
Saratov
Penza
Ul'yanovsk
Kazan
Tol'yatti
Ufa
Nizhniy Tagil
Sverdlovsk
Tyumen
Chelyabinsk
Kurgan
Magnitogorsk
Petropavlovsk
Omsk
Tomsk
Novosibirsk
Keme
Prokopyevsk
Novokuznetsk
Barnaul
Pavlodar
Semipalatinsk
ALT

Kuybyshev
Orenburg
Ural'sk
Orsk
Aktyubinsk
Kustanay
Karaganda
Mt. Belukf 4506

Don
Volga
Engels
Volgograd
Astrakhan
Ural
Guryev

BLACK SEA
Stavropol'
Ordzhonikidze
Groznyy
Makhachkala
Elbrus 5633
CAUCASUS
Batumi
TURKEY
Tbilisi
Baku
Mt. Ararat 5165
Tabriz
ZAGROS MTS
ELBURZ MTS
Tehran
Mashhad
Esfahan
IRAN

ARAL SEA
Syr Darya
Amu Darya
Lake Balkhash
Chimkent
Tashkent
Frunze
Alma-Ata
Uru
Chardzhou
Ashkhabad
Bukhara
Leninabad
Samarkand
Andizhan
Osh
Hantengri Feng 7439
Dushanbe
Communism Peak 7495
AFGHANISTAN

U R A L   M T S
Ob
Yenisei
Irtysh

0°
20°
50°
40°
40°
30°

60° 80°

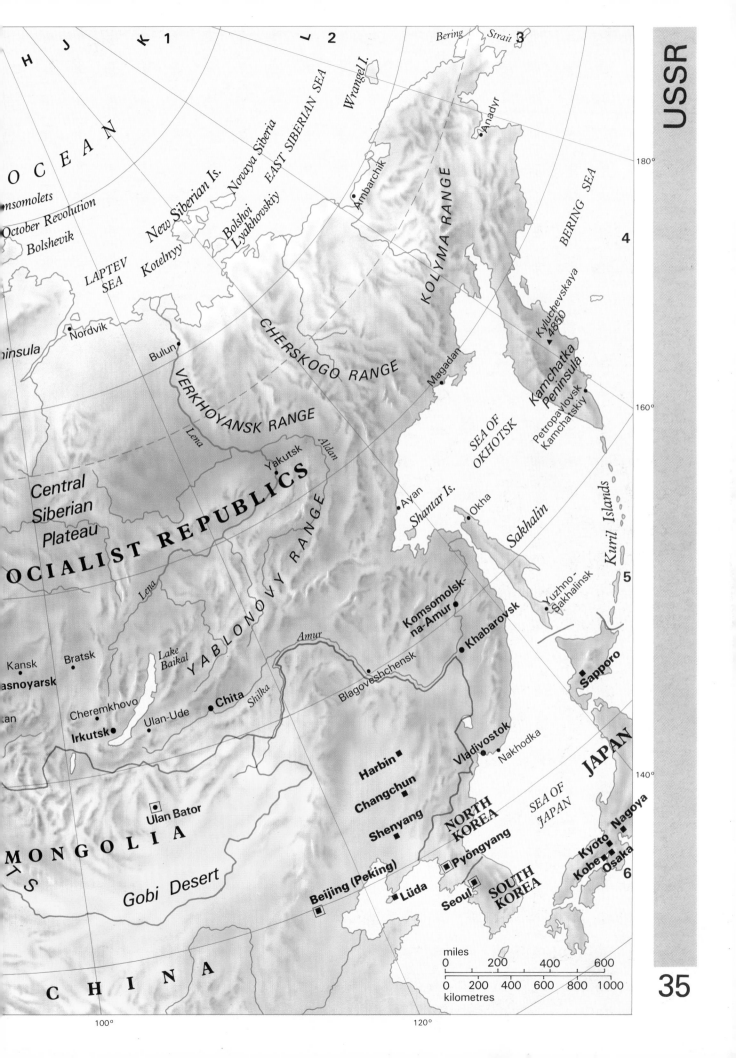

H J K **1** L **2** **3**

Bering *Strait*

OCEAN

omsomolets
October Revolution
Bolshevik

New Siberian Is.

Novaya Siberia

Bolshoi Lyakhovskiy

EAST SIBERIAN SEA

Wrangel I.

Ambarchik

Anadyr

4

LAPTEV SEA

Kotelnyy

BERING SEA

insula

Nordvik

Bulun

CHERSKOGO RANGE

KOLYMA RANGE

Magadan

Kyluchevskaya
4850

Kamchatka Peninsula

180°

160°

VERKHOYANSK RANGE

Lena

Aldan

Yakutsk

SEA OF
OKHOTSK

Petropavlovsk
Kamchatskiy

Central
Siberian
Plateau

OCIALIST REPUBLICS

Ayan

Shantar Is.

Okha

Sakhalin

Kuril Islands

Lena

YABLONOVY RANGE

Yuzhno-
Sakhalinsk

5

Kansk

Bratsk

Lake Baikal

Amur

**Komsomolsk-
na-Amur**

Khabarovsk

asnoyarsk

Cheremkhovo

Ulan-Ude

Chita

Shilka

Blagoveshchensk

Sapporo

kan

Irkutsk

Vladivostok

Nakhodka

Harbin

140°

Changchun

SEA OF
JAPAN

JAPAN

Ulan Bator

Shenyang

**NORTH
KOREA**

Kyoto **Nagoya**

M O N G O L I A

Pyŏngyang

Kobe
Osaka

6

Gobi Desert

Beijing (Peking)

Lüda

Seoul

**SOUTH
KOREA**

TS

miles
0   200   400   600

C H I N A

0   200   400   600   800   1000
kilometres

35

100°   120°

THE MIDDLE EAST

Edirne **A** **Istanbul** B • Sinop C Batumi D **CAUCASUS MTS** E

BLACK SEA

Gallipoli
Sea of Marmara
Izmit
Adapazari
Samsun
PONTINE MTS
Tbilisi
Kirovabad

Bursa
Ankara
Sivas
Yerevan

Eskisehir
Erzurum
Mt Ararat 5165

TURKEY
Kizil
Diyarbakir
Lake Van
Siirt
Rezaiyeh
Lake Urmia
Tabriz

Izmir
Afyon
Lake Tuz
Konya
Kayseri
Malatya
Mardin
Marāgheh

Mt Erciyas 3916
Maras
Urfa
Erbil
Hamadā

Rhodes
TAURUS MTS
Adana
Gaziantep
Mosul

Mersin
Halab
Kirkuk

Antakya
Latakia
SYRIA
CYPRUS
Nicosia
Hama
Euphrates
Qahremānsha

MEDITERRANEAN SEA
Tripoli
Homs
Tigris
Tharthar Basin

Beirut
Damascus
IRAQ
Baghdad
Khorrama

LEBANON
Haifa
Irbid
Syrian
Karbala
Hilla

Tel-Aviv-Yafo
Zarqa
Amman
Desert
An Najaf

ISRAEL
Jerusalem
Hor al Hammar
Ahva

Matruh
Port Said
Dead Sea
Khorran

Alexandria
Suez Canal
JORDAN
Basra
Aba

El Mahalla el Kubra
El Mansura
KUWAIT
Kuwa

Tanta
Suez
Elat

El Giza
Cairo
Al Jawf

Beni Suef
Tabūk
An Nafud
Hafar

El Minya
Hail

Asyūt
Gebel Katherina 2637

EGYPT
Nile
Al KH

Luxor
Ramah

Aswân
Medina
Riyadh

Yanbu'al Bahr

Lake Nasser

SAUDI

Wadi Halfa
Nubian
ARABIA

Dongola
Desert
Jiddah
Mecca

At Tā'if

SUDAN
Port Sudan
Rub

Suakin

Jizān

Khartoum North
Omdurman **Khartoum**
Kassala
Massawa
YEMEN

Wad Medani
Asmara
Sana
SOUTHE
YEME

Sennar
Hodeida

ETHIOPIA
Taizz

Aden

40°
35°
30°
25°
20°
15°

35°
40°
45°

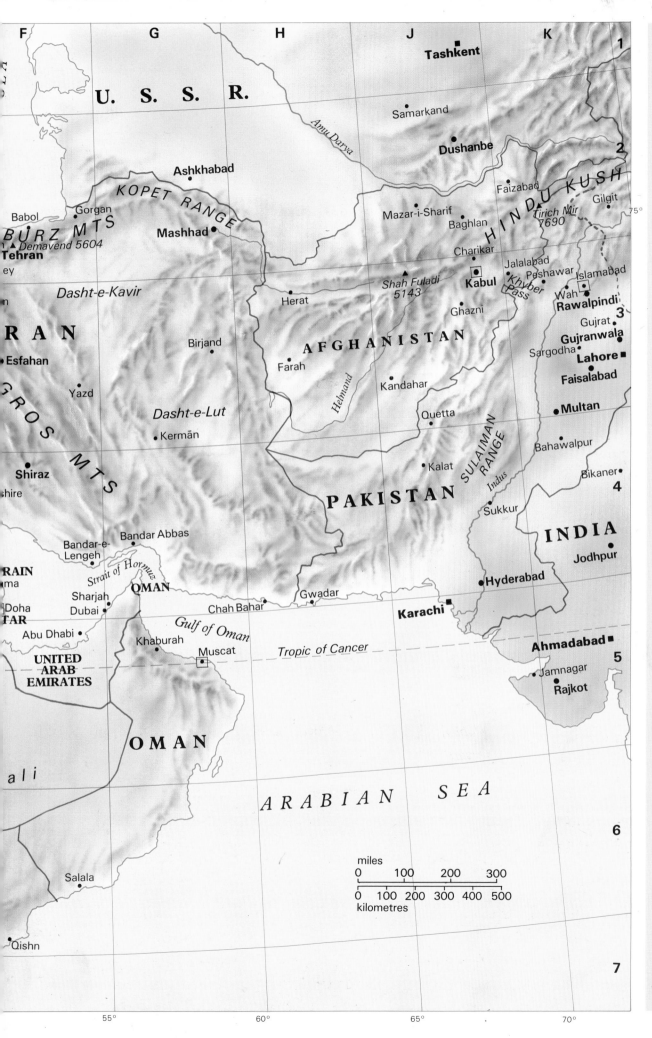

F G H J K

1

U. S. S. R.

Tashkent

Samarkand

Dushanbe

Amu Darya

2

Ashkhabad

KOPET RANGE

Faizabad

HINDU KUSH

Gilgit

75°

Babol

Gorgan

Mazar-i-Sharif

Baghlan

Tirich Mir
7690

BURZ MTS

Demavend 5604

Mashhad

Charikar

Jalalabad

Peshawar

Islamabad

Tehran

Dasht-e-Kavir

Shah Fuladi
5143

Kabul

Khyber
Pass

Wah

Rawalpindi

3

ey

Herat

Ghazni

Gujrat

Gujranwala

RAN

Birjand

Sargodha

Lahore

Esfahan

Farah

AFGHANISTAN

Faisalabad

Yazd

Kandahar

GROS MTS

Dasht-e-Lut

Kerman

Quetta

Multan

Bahawalpur

Kalat

SULAIMAN RANGE

Indus

Bikaner

Shiraz

PAKISTAN

4

shire

Sukkur

INDIA

Bandar-e-
Lengeh

Bandar Abbas

Jodhpur

RAIN

Strait of Hormuz

ma

OMAN

Hyderabad

Sharjah

Dubai

Gwadar

Doha

Chah Bahar

Karachi

TAR

Gulf of Oman

Abu Dhabi

Khaburah

Ahmadabad

UNITED
ARAB
EMIRATES

Muscat

Tropic of Cancer

5

Jamnagar

Rajkot

OMAN

ali

ARABIAN SEA

Salala

6

miles

0   100   200   300

0 100 200 300 400 500
kilometres

Qishn

7

55°   60°   65°   70°

A B C D

35°

HINDU KUSH
KARAKORAM RANGE
Gilgit
K2 8611
Karakoram Pass

Herat
Charikar
Jalalabad
Nanga Parbat 8126
Leh
Kabul
Khyber Pass
Peshawar
Ghazni
Wah
Islamabad
Srinagar
Rawalpindi

AFGHANISTAN

Birjand

Jammu
Gujrat
Sialkot
Farah
Sargodha
Gujranwala
Lahore
Amritsar
Jullundur
Helmand
Faisalabad
Kandahar
Ludhiana
Chandigarh
Nanda
Sahiwal
Patiala
Dehra Dun
30°
Multan
Ambala
Saharanpur
Quetta
Bahawalpur
Meerut
Moradabad
Rohtak
Delhi
Rampur
IRAN
PAKISTAN
Kalat
New Delhi
Aligarh
Barei
SULAIMAN RANGE
Alwar
Shahja
Indus
Bikaner
Mathura
Agra
Lucknow
Sukkur
Jaipur
Khairpur
Jodhpur
Ajmer
Gwalior
Kanpu
Chah Bahar
25°
Kota
Jhansi
Allah
Gwadar
Hyderabad
Udaipur
IND
Tropic of Cancer
Karachi
Ahmadabad
Ratlam
Ujjain
Bhopal
Jab
Jamnagar
Indore
Rajkot
Vadodara
Bhavnagar
Surat
20°
Jalgaon
Nagpur
Gulf of Cambay
Malegaon
Akola
Nasik
Nander
60°
Bombay
Ahmadnagar
Pune
Deccan
Warangal
ARABIAN SEA
Sholapur
Hyderabad
Vijaya
Kolhapur
WESTERN GHATS
Kurnool
Guntur
15°
Belgaum
Machilipa
Hubli
EASTERN
Nel
GHATS
Bangalore
Ma
Mangalore
Mysore
Calicut
Salem
Cudda
10°
Coimbatore
Tiruchchira
Lakshadweep Is. (India)
Cochin
Madurai
Alleppey
miles
0 100 200 300 400
0 100 200 300 400 500 600
kilometres
Tuticorin
Trivandrum
Trincoma
Nagercoil
Ja
SRI LANKA
Colombo
Galle

65° 70° 75° 80°

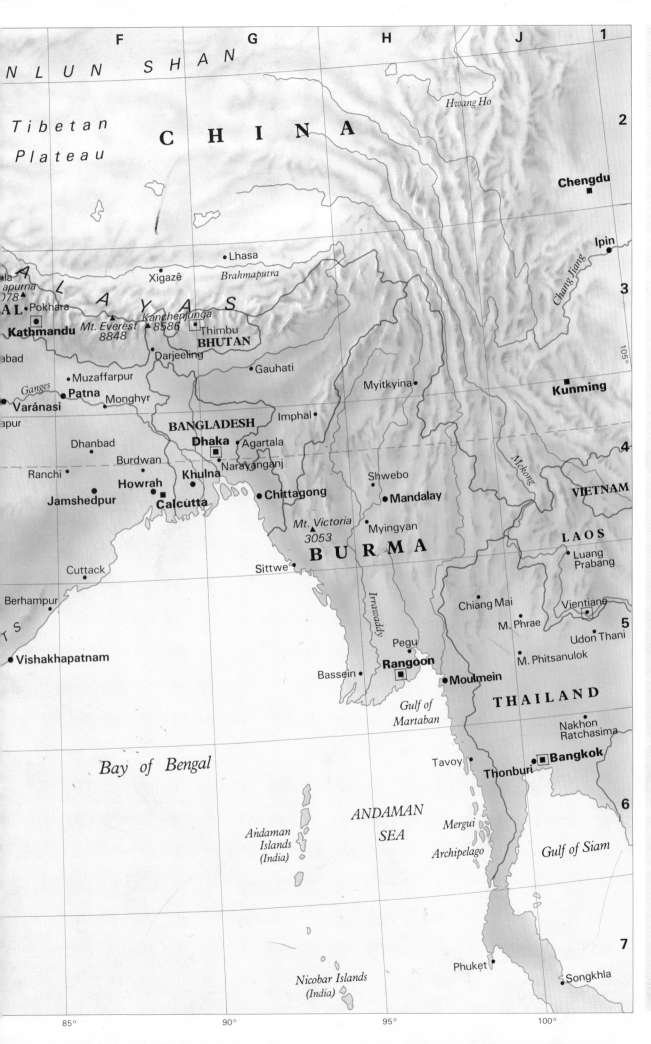

NLUN SHANG

Tibetan
Plateau

CHINA

Hwang Ho

Chengdu

Ipin

Chang Jiang

105°

Lhasa
Xigazê   *Brahmaputra*

apurna
078

AL   Pokhara

Kathmandu   Mt. Everest   Kanchenjunga   8586   Thimbu
8848   BHUTAN

Darjeeling

Gauhati

Myitkyina

Kunming

abad

Ganges   Muzaffarpur

Patna   Monghyr

Varánasi

Imphal

BANGLADESH

apur

Dhanbad

Dhaka   Agartala

Burdwan   Narayanganj

Ranchi   Khulna

Shwebo

Howrah

Chittagong

Mandalay

Jamshedpur   Calcutta

Mt. Victoria
3053   Myingyan

VIETNAM

LAOS

Luang
Prabang

BURMA

Cuttack

Sittwe

Irrawaddy

Chiang Mai

Vientiane

M. Phrae

Berhampur

TS

Udon Thani

M. Phitsanulok

Pegu

Vishakhapatnam

Bassein

Rangoon

Moulmein

THAILAND

*Gulf of
Martaban*

Nakhon
Ratchasima

Bay of Bengal

Tavoy

Thonburi

Bangkok

*ANDAMAN
SEA*

*Andaman
Islands
(India)*

Mergui

Archipelago

Gulf of Siam

Phuket

*Nicobar Islands
(India)*

Songkhla

85°   90°   95°   100°

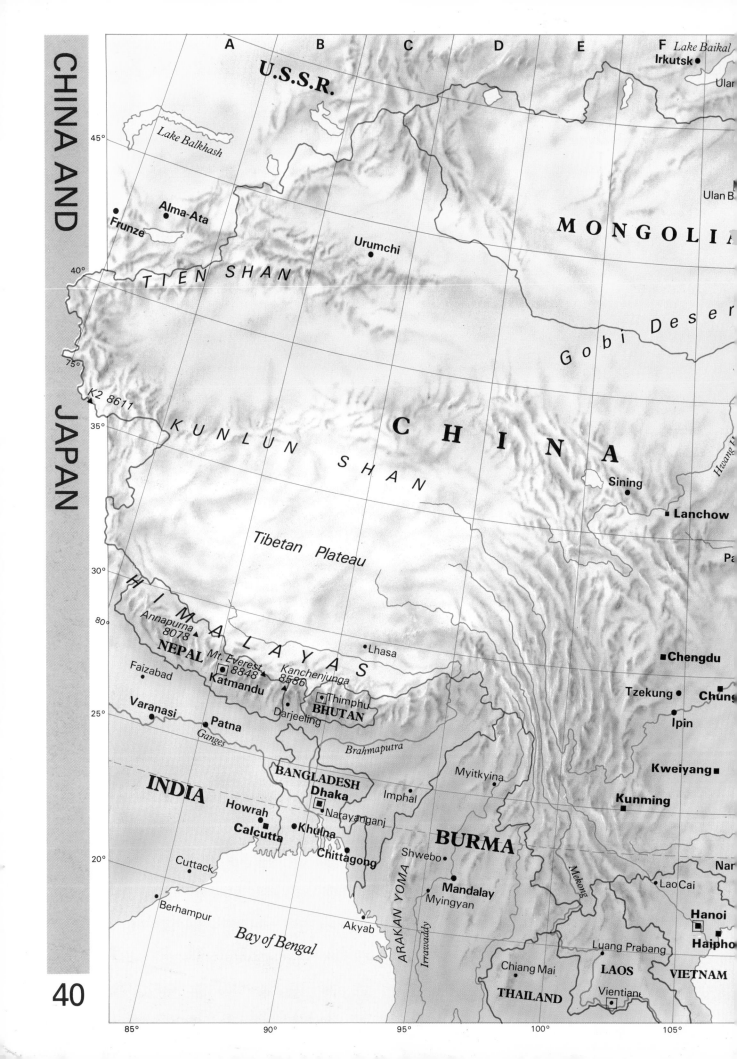

A   B   C   D   E   F

U.S.S.R.

Lake Baikal
Irkutsk
Ular
Ulan B.

45°

Lake Balkhash

Alma-Ata
Frunze

M O N G O L I A

Urumchi

40°

T I E N   S H A N

Gobi Deser

75°

K2 8611

K U N L U N   S H A N

35°

C H I N A

Sining

Hwang H

Lanchow

Pa

Tibetan Plateau

30°

H I

Annapurna
8078 ▲

80°

M

NEPAL

Mt. Everest
■ 8848 ▲

Faizabad

Katmandu

A

Kanchenjunga
8586 ▲

L

Lhasa

■ **Chengdu**

Tzekung ●   **Chung**

Varanasi

A

Darjeeling

Thimphu
BHUTAN

Ipin

25°

Patna

Y

A

S

Ganges

Brahmaputra

Kweiyang ■

INDIA

BANGLADESH

Myitkyina

Dhaka
Narayanganj

Imphal

Kunming

Howrah ■

Calcutta

Khulna

Chittagong

BURMA

Shwebo

20°

Cuttack

Nar

Lao Cai

Mandalay

Myingyan

Mekong

Berhampur

Akyab

ARAKAN YOMA

Irrawaddy

Hanoi

Haipho

Bay of Bengal

Luang Prabang

Chiang Mai

LAOS

VIETNAM

THAILAND

Vientiane

85°   90°   95°   100°   105°

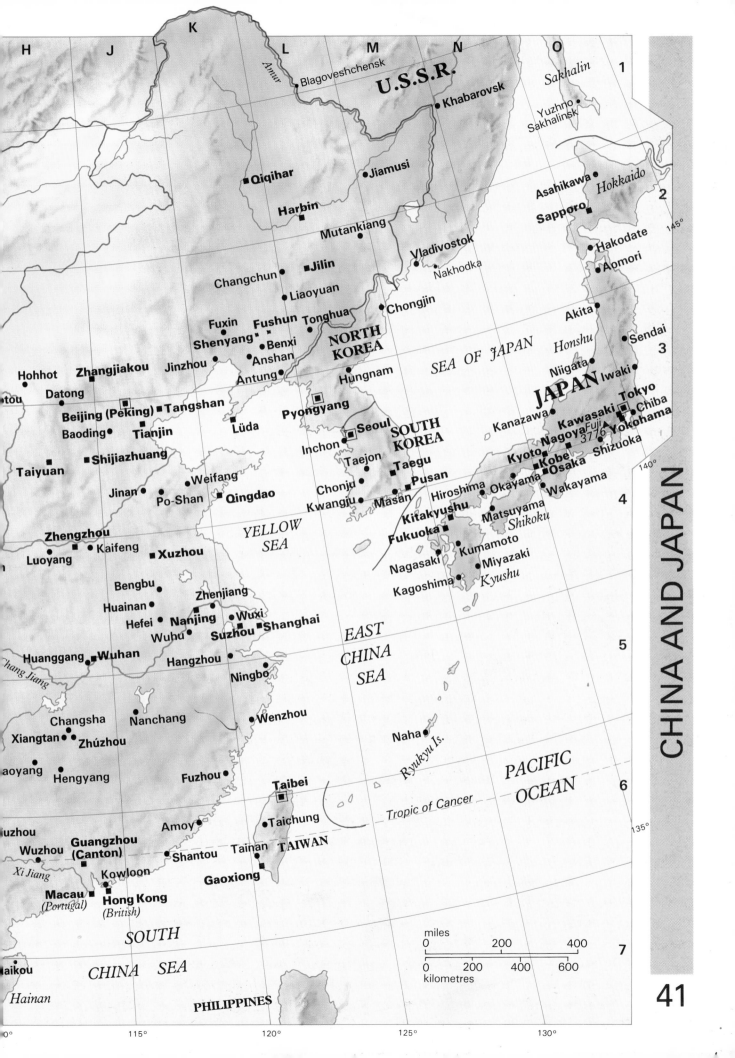

H   J   K   L   M   N   O

Amur Blagoveshchensk   1
U.S.S.R.   *Sakhalin*

● **Khabarovsk**   Yuzhno-
                                Sakhalinsk

● **Qiqihar**   ● Jiamusi   Asahikawa ●   *Hokkaido*   2
                                Sapporo ■

● **Harbin**   Hakodate ●   145°

Mutankiang   Aomori ●

                Vladivostok   Akita ●
Changchun ● **Jilin**   ● Nakhodka   *Honshu*   Sendai ●   3

● Liaoyuan   ● Chongjin   Niigata ● Iwaki ●

● Fuxin **Fushun** Tonghua **NORTH**   **SEA OF JAPAN**   **JAPAN**
● Shenyang ■ ● Benxi **KOREA**   Tokyo ●
Hohhot ● **Zhangjiakou** Jinzhou ● Anshan   Kanazawa ● **Kawasaki** Chiba ■
tou Datong ● Antung   ● Hungnam   **Nagoya** *Fuji* **Yokohama** ■
Beijing (Peking) ■ ● **Tangshan** □ Pyongyang   **Kyoto** 3776 ● Shizuoka
Baoding ● **Tianjin** Lüda ■   □ **Seoul** **SOUTH**   **Kobe** ● ● Shizuoka   140°
Taiyuan ■ **Shijiazhuang** ● Inchon Taejon **KOREA**   **Osaka** ■ Wakayama
                ● Chonju **Taegu**   Hiroshima ● Okayama ●
Jinan ● Weifang ●   Kwangju ● Masan ● **Pusan** **Kitakyushu** Matsuyama ● *Shikoku*   4
Zhengzhou ● Po-Shan ● **Qingdao** ■   **Fukuoka** ■
Luoyang ● Kaifeng ●   Nagasaki ● Kumamoto ● Miyazaki ●
  Xuzhou ■   Kagoshima ● *Kyushu*

YELLOW
SEA

Bengbu ●
Huainan ● Zhenjiang ●
Hefei ● **Nanjing** ● Wuxi ●   **EAST**   5
Wuhu ● **Suzhou** ■ **Shanghai** ■   **CHINA**
Huanggang ● **Wuhan** ■ Hangzhou ●   **SEA**
Chang Jiang   Ningbo ●

Changsha ● Nanchang ●   Wenzhou ●
Xiangtan ● **Zhúzhou** ●   Naha ●   **PACIFIC**   6
aoyang ● Hengyang ●   Fuzhou ●   *Ryukyu Is.* **OCEAN**
                Taibei □   Tropic of Cancer

iuzhou ●   Amoy ● ● Taichung
Wuzhou ● **Guangzhou**   Tainan ● **TAIWAN**
  (Canton) Shantou ●
Xi Jiang Kowloon ● **Gaoxiong** ■
Macau ■ **Hong Kong**
(Portugal) *(British)*

SOUTH   miles   7
aikou ●   0   200   400
CHINA SEA   0 200 400 600
Hainan   kilometres

PHILIPPINES   **41**

0°   115°   120°   125°   130°

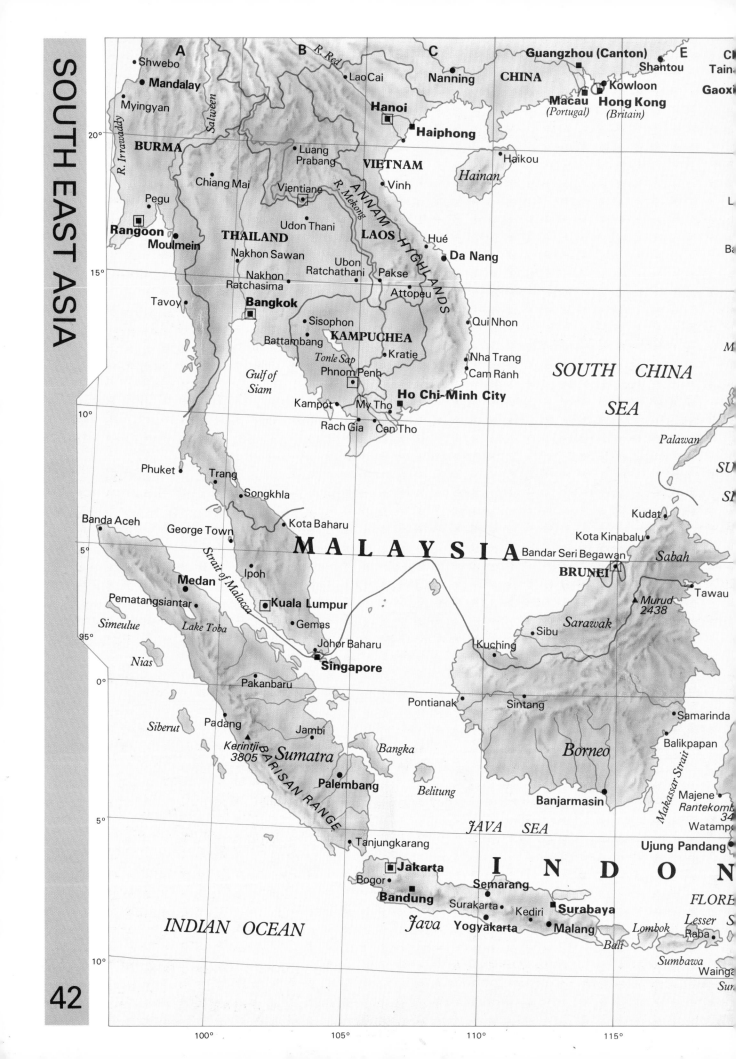

A   B   R. Red   C   E

- Shwebo
- **Mandalay**
- Myingyan

Salween

BURMA

R. Irrawaddy

- Lao Cai
- Nanning

CHINA

- **Guangzhou (Canton)**
- Shantou
- Tainan

Hanoi
- Kowloon
- **Macau**   Hong Kong
- (Portugal)   (Britain)
- Gaoxi

- **Haiphong**

- Luang
  Prabang

VIETNAM

- Haikou

- Chiang Mai
- Vientiane
- Vinh

Hainan

R. Mekong

ANNAM HIGHLANDS

- Pegu

Rangoon
- Moulmein

THAILAND

- Udon Thani

LAOS

- Hué
- **Da Nang**

- Nakhon Sawan
- Ubon
  Ratchathani
- Pakse
- Attopeu

- Nakhon
  Ratchasima

- Tavoy

Bangkok

- Sisophon

- Qui Nhon

KAMPUCHEA

- Battambang
- Kratie
- Nha Trang
- Cam Ranh

Tonle Sap

*Gulf of
Siam*

Phnom Penh

- **Ho Chi-Minh City**

SOUTH CHINA

- Kampot
- My Tho

- Rach Gia
- Can Tho

SEA

Palawan

- Phuket
- Trang

- Songkhla

SU

SI

- Banda Aceh

- George Town
- Kota Baharu

- Kudat

- Kota Kinabalu

M A L A Y S I A

Bandar Seri Begawan

Sabah

- Ipoh

BRUNEI

- Tawau

Strait of Malacca

- **Medan**

- Pematangsiantar

Simeulue

Lake Toba

▲ Murud
2438

- Kuala Lumpur
- Gemas

Sarawak

- Sibu

Nias

- Johor Baharu
- Kuching

Singapore

- Pakanbaru

Siberut

- Padang
- Jambi

- Pontianak
- Sintang

Borneo

- Samarinda

- Balikpapan

Kerintji
3805

BARISAN RANGE

Sumatra

Palembang

Bangka

Belitung

- Banjarmasin

Makassar Strait

- Majene

*Rantekomb
34

*Watamp

JAVA SEA

- Tanjungkarang

- Ujung Pandang

I N D O N

- □ **Jakarta**
- Bogor
- Semarang

FLORE

- **Bandung**
- Surakarta
- Kediri
- **Surabaya**

Lesser S

INDIAN OCEAN

Java   Yogyakarta   Malang

- Raba

Bali

Sumbawa

Lombok

- Waing

100°   105°   110°   115°

20°
15°
10°
5°
95°
0°
5°
10°

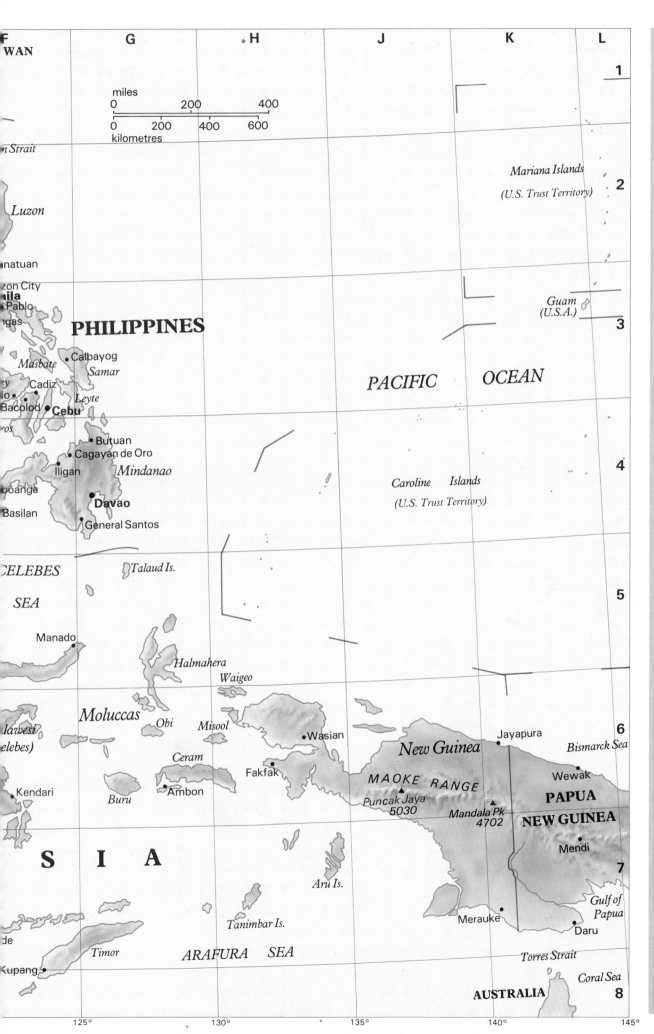

F   **G**   **H**   **J**   **K**   **L**

WAN

miles
0   200   400

0   200   400   600
kilometres

1

n Strait

Mariana Islands

(U.S. Trust Territory)

2

Luzon

natuan

zon City
ila
Pablo
gas

PHILIPPINES

Masbate • Calbayog
Samar

Guam
(U.S.A.)

3

y • Cadiz
Bacolod • **Cebu**
Leyte

PACIFIC   OCEAN

ros

• Butuan
• Cagayan de Oro
Iligan •   *Mindanao*

Caroline   Islands

4

boanga
Basilan

Davao
• General Santos

(U.S. Trust Territory)

CELEBES

SEA

Talaud Is.

5

Manado •

Halmahera

Waigeo

Moluccas   *Obi*

Misool

Jayapura •

6

lawesi
elebes)

• Wasian

New Guinea

Bismarck Sea

Ceram

Fakfak •

MAOKE   RANGE

Wewak •

Kendari •

Buru   • Ambon

Puncak Jaya ▲
5030

Mandala Pk ▲
4702

PAPUA

NEW GUINEA

S   I   A

• Mendi

7

Aru Is.

Tanimbar Is.

Merauke •

*Gulf of
Papua*

• Daru

de

Timor

ARAFURA   SEA

Torres Strait

Kupang •

Coral Sea

AUSTRALIA

8

125°   130°   135°   140°   145°

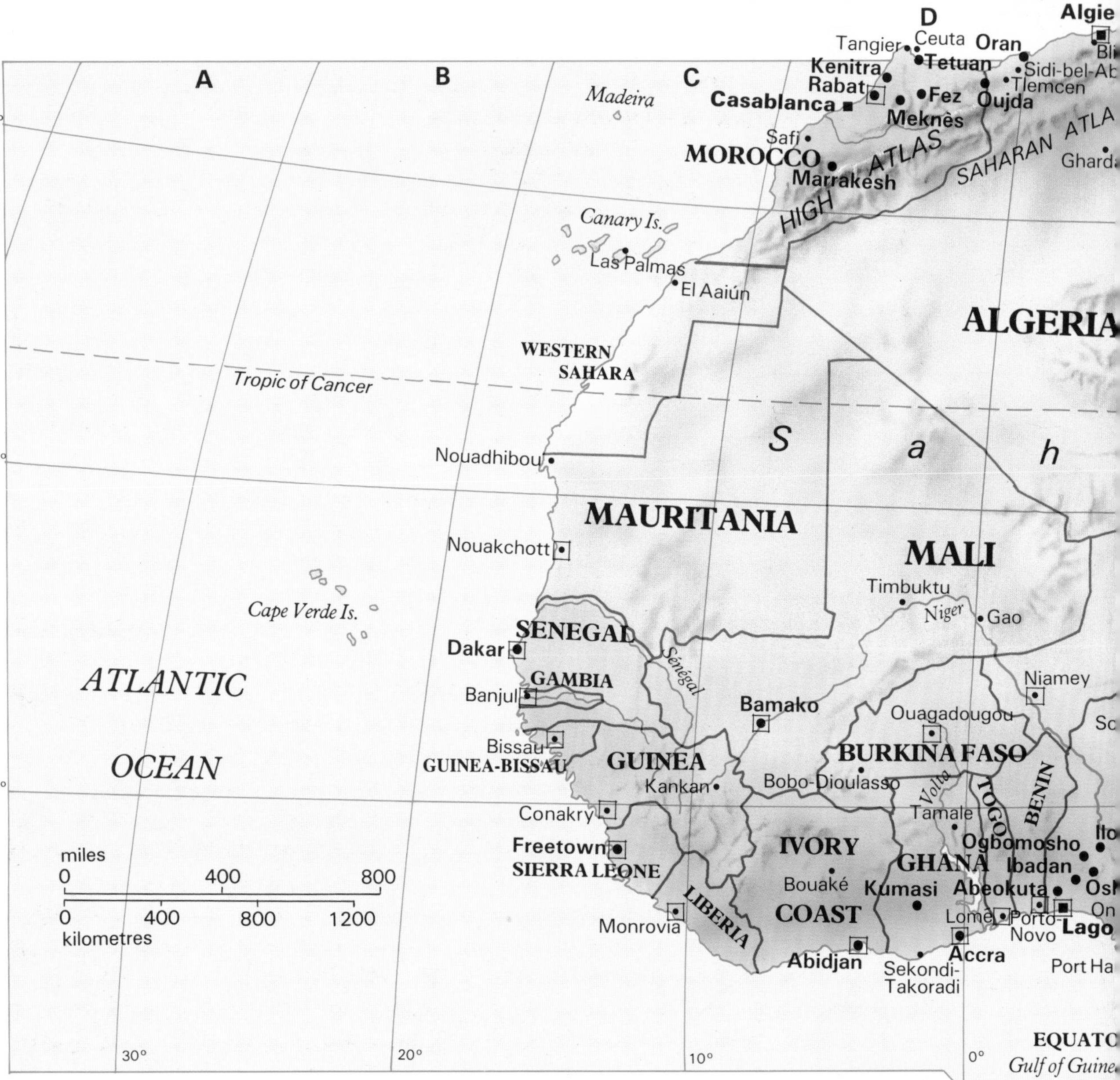

Top map (West Africa)

A   B   C   D

Algie

Madeira

Tangier   Ceuta   **Oran**
Kenitra   **Tetuan**   Bli
Rabat   Sidi-bel-Ab
Casablanca   **Fez**   **Oujda**   Tlemcen

30°

Safi   **Meknès**

MOROCCO   ATLAS   SAHARAN ATLA

Marrakesh   HIGH   Ghard

Canary Is.

ALGERIA

Las Palmas

El Aaiún

Tropic of Cancer

**WESTERN
SAHARA**

S   *a*   *h*

20°

Nouadhibou

MAURITANIA   **MALI**

Nouakchott

Timbuktu

Niger   Gao

Cape Verde Is.

SENEGAL   Niamey

Dakar   *Sénégal*   So

GAMBIA   Ouagadougou

Banjul   **BURKINA FASO**

ATLANTIC   Bamako

Bissau   **BENIN**

GUINEA-BISSAU   **GUINEA**   *Volta*   **TOGO**

OCEAN   Kankan   Bobo-Dioulasso

10°

Conakry   Tamale   **Ogbomosho**   Ilo

Freetown   **IVORY**   **GHANA**   Ibadan   Osh

SIERRA LEONE   Bouaké   **Kumasi**   **Abeokuta**   On

COAST   Lome   Porto   **Lago**

LIBERIA   Novo

Monrovia   **Accra**

Sekondi-   Port Ha
Takoradi

Abidjan

miles
0   400   800

0   400   800   1200
kilometres

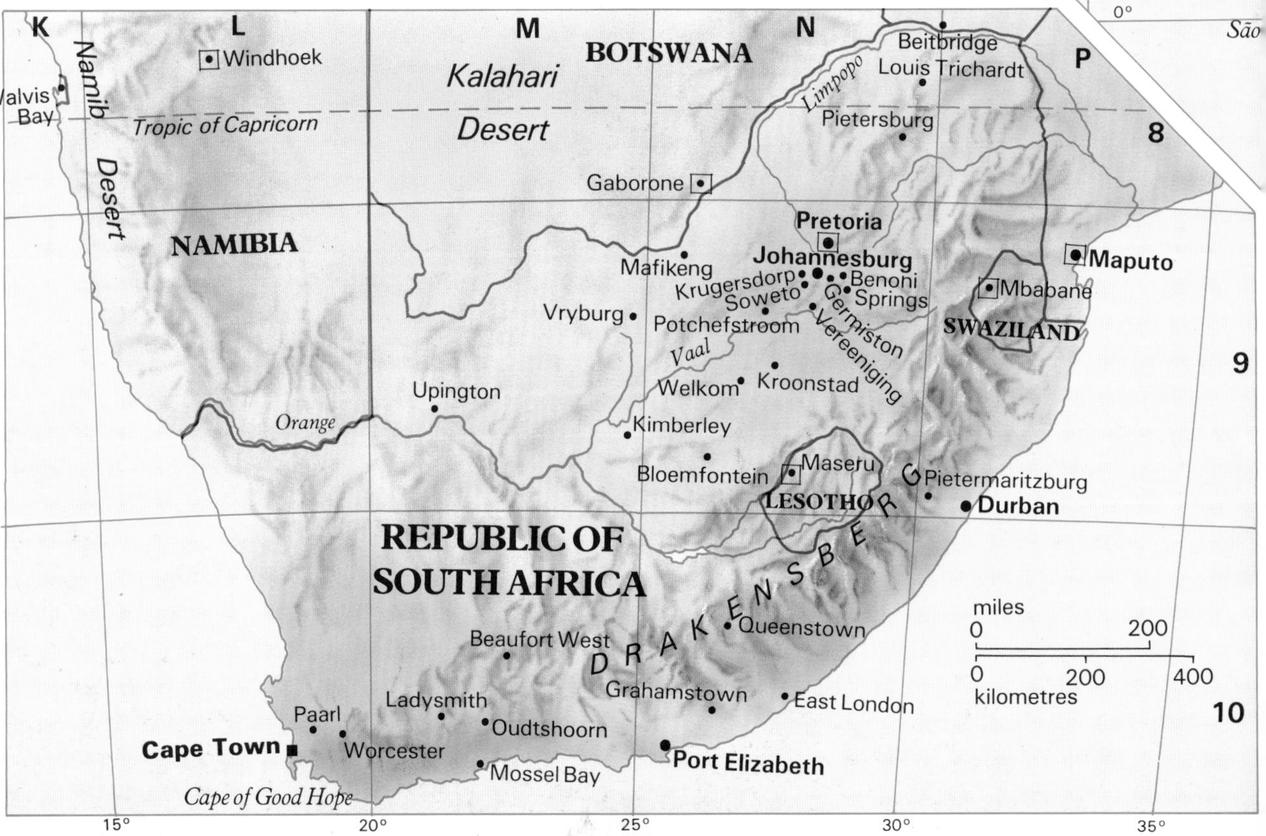

EQUATO

Gulf of Guine

0°   *São*

30°   20°   10°   0°

Bottom map (Southern Africa)

K   L   M   N   P

Namib   **Windhoek**   **BOTSWANA**

Walvis   *Kalahari*   Beitbridge
Bay   Louis Trichardt

Tropic of Capricorn   *Desert*   *Limpopo*

8

Pietersburg

25°

Desert   Gaborone

NAMIBIA   **Pretoria**   **Maputo**

Johannesburg

Mafikeng   Krugersdorp   Benoni   Mbabane
Soweto   Springs
Germiston

Vryburg   Potchefstroom   Vereeniging   **SWAZILAND**

Vaal   **9**

Upington   Welkom   Kroonstad

Orange

Kimberley

Maseru   Pietermaritzburg

Bloemfontein   **Durban**

LESOTHO

30°

**REPUBLIC OF
SOUTH AFRICA**   DRAKENSBERG

Queenstown   miles
0   200

Beaufort West   0   200   400
kilometres

Grahamstown   East London

Ladysmith   **10**

Paarl   Oudtshoorn

Cape Town   Worcester   **Port Elizabeth**

Mossel Bay

Cape of Good Hope

15°   20°   25°   30°   35°

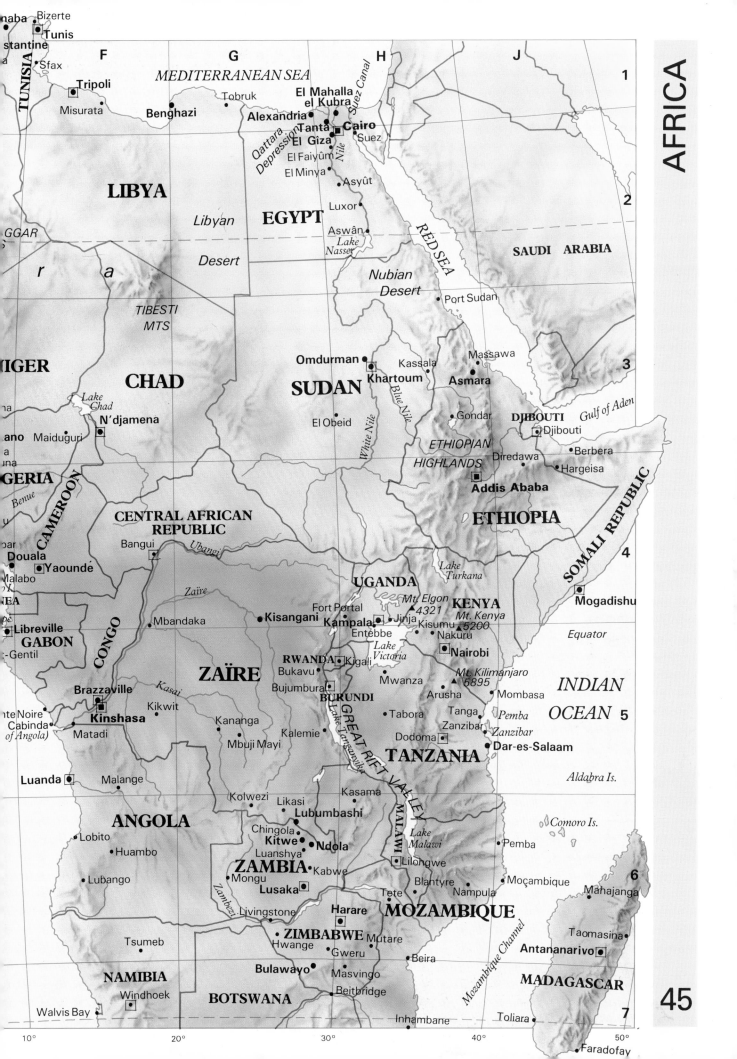

naba
Bizerte
Tunis
stantine
a
Sfax
TUNISIA

F

G

MEDITERRANEAN SEA

H

Tobruk

J

1

Tripoli
Misurata
Benghazi

El Mahalla
el Kubra
Alexandria
Tanta **Cairo**
Suez

El Giza
El Faiyûm

Qattara Depression

Suez Canal

LIBYA

Libyan

EGYPT

El Minya

Luxor

2

GGAR

r   a

Desert

Aswân
Lake Nasser

SAUDI ARABIA

RED SEA

Nubian Desert

Port Sudan

TIBESTI MTS

IGER

CHAD

Lake Chad
N'djamena

Omdurman
Khartoum

Kassala

Massawa

3

SUDAN

Asmara

lano   Maiduguri
a
una

El Obeid

Gondar

DJIBOUTI
Djibouti

Gulf of Aden

Berbera
Hargeisa

GERIA

Benue

CAMEROON

CENTRAL AFRICAN REPUBLIC

Bangui

Ubangi

White Nile

Blue Nile

ETHIOPIAN HIGHLANDS

Diredawa

Addis Ababa

SOMALI REPUBLIC

4

Douala
Malabo
EA

Yaounde

Zaïre

ETHIOPIA

Mogadishu

Libreville
GABON
-Gentil

CONGO

Mbandaka

Kisangani

Lake Turkana

UGANDA
Fort Portal
Kampala Jinji
Entèbbe

Mt Elgon
▲4321

KENYA
Kisumu
Mt Kenya
▲5200
Nakuru

Equator

INDIAN

Kasai

ZAÏRE

RWANDA
Bukavu   Kigali
Bujumbura
BURUNDI

Lake Victoria

Mwanza

Nairobi

Mt Kilimanjaro
▲5895

Arusha

Mombasa

OCEAN 5

Brazzaville
nte Noire
Cabinda
(of Angola)
Kinshasa
Matadi

Kikwit

Kananga

Mbuji Mayi

Kalemie

Lake Tanganyika

GREAT RIFT VALLEY

Tabora
Dodoma

TANZANIA

Tanga
Pemba
Zanzibar
Zanzibar
Dar-es-Salaam

Aldabra Is.

Luanda
Malange

Kolwezi Likasi

Kasama

Comoro Is.

ANGOLA

Lobito
Huambo

Lubango

Chingola
Kitwe
Luanshya
ZAMBIA
Mongu

Lubumbashi

Ndola

Kabwe

Lake Malawi

MALAWI

Pemba

6

Lusaka
Livingstone

Zambezi

Tete

Lilongwe
Blantyre

Nampula

Moçambique

Mahajanga

Harare
Tsumeb
ZIMBABWE
Hwange   Mutare
Gweru

Beira

Mozambique Channel

Taomasina

Antananarivo

NAMIBIA
Windhoek
BOTSWANA

Bulawayo

Masvingo
Beitbridge

MOZAMBIQUE

MADAGASCAR

Walvis Bay

Inhambane

Toliara

7

Faradofay

10°

20°

30°

40°

50°

CANADA

A **B** **C** **D** **E** **F**

65° 70°

ALASKA RANGE
Mt. McKinley
6194
Yukon
Fairbanks

ALASKA (U.S.A.)

Anchorage
150°
Seward

Gulf of Alaska

Dawson

YUKON

MACKENZIE MTS

Mt. Logan
6050

Whitehorse

Skagway

Juneau

PACIFIC

OCEAN

140°
55°

Queen
Charlotte Is.

COASTAL

MTS

R O C K Y

Fort St. John

Prince George

BRITISH
COLUMBIA

SELKIRK

130°

Vancouver I.

Vancouver

Seattle
Tacoma
Mt St. Helens
WASHINGTON
Spokane
MTS

Portland
Salem

OREGON

Snake

IDAHO
Boise

UNITED

STATES

OF

AMERICA

40°

CALIFORNIA

Sacramento · Reno
Oakland
San Francisco

NEVADA

Ogden
Salt Lake City
Provo

UTAH

BEAUFORT
SEA

Banks I.

Mc Clure Strait
Melville I.

Viscount Melv
Sound

Prince o
Wales I.

Mc Clintock
Channel

Amundsen
Gulf

Victoria
Island

Coppermine

Bathurst Inlet

Great Bear
Lake

Mackenzie

NORTHWEST

TERRITORIES

Yellowknife
Fort Reliance

Great
Slave Lake

Eskimo Po

C

A

N

Church

MANITOB

ALBERTA

Edmonton

SASKATCHEWAN

Saskatchewan

Saskatoon

Calgary

Lethbridge

Moose Jaw

Regina

Lake
Winnipeg

Brandon
Winnipeg

Ke

Great Falls

MONTANA

Billings

NORTH DAKOTA

Bismarck

Fargo

MINNES

SOUTH DAKOTA

Pierre

Minneapo
St.

Sioux Falls

Missouri

WYOMING

Cheyenne

NEBRASKA

COLORADO

AMERICA

Sioux C

IO

50°

45°

120° 110° 100°

46

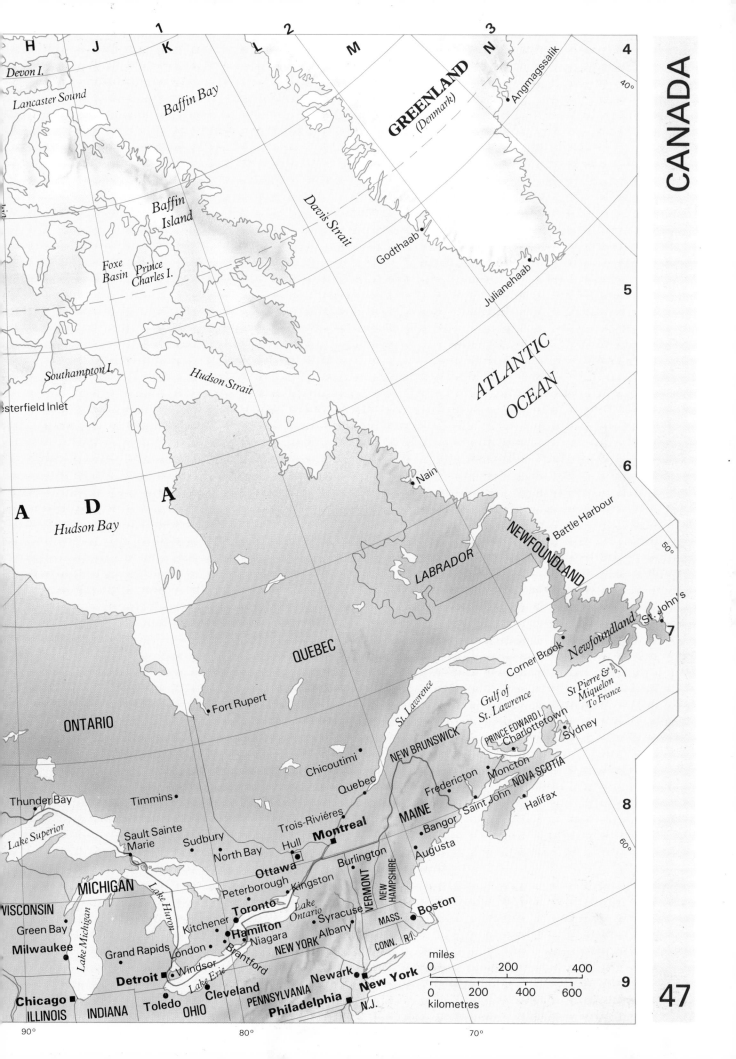

H   J   K   L   M   N
1   2   3   4

40°

Devon I.

Lancaster Sound

Baffin Bay

GREENLAND
(Denmark)

Angmagssalik

Baffin
Island

Davis Strait

Foxe
Basin   Prince
Charles I.

Godthaab

5

Julianehaab

Southampton I.

Hudson Strait

ATLANTIC
OCEAN

esterfield Inlet

Nain

6

50°

A   D   A

Hudson Bay

NEWFOUNDLAND

Battle Harbour

LABRADOR

Corner Brook

Newfoundland   St. John's

7

QUEBEC

St Pierre &
Miquelon
To France

Fort Rupert

Gulf of
St. Lawrence   PRINCE EDWARD I.
Charlottetown   Sydney

St. Lawrence

ONTARIO

Chicoutimi

NEW BRUNSWICK

Fredericton   Moncton   NOVA SCOTIA

Quebec

Thunder Bay   Timmins

Trois-Riviéres   MAINE   Saint John   Halifax

8

60°

Lake Superior   Sault Sainte
Marie   Sudbury

Hull   Montreal

Bangor

Augusta

North Bay

Ottawa   Burlington

MICHIGAN

Peterborough   Kingston

VERMONT

WISCONSIN

Toronto

Lake
Ontario   Syracuse

NEW
HAMPSHIRE

Boston

Green Bay

Kitchener

Hamilton

Albany

MASS.

Milwaukee   Grand Rapids   London   Brantford   Niagara

NEW YORK

CONN.   R.I.

miles
0   200   400

Windsor

Newark   New York

Detroit

Lake Erie   Cleveland   PENNSYLVANIA

0   200   400   600

9

Chicago   Toledo   OHIO   Philadelphia   N.J.   kilometres

ILLINOIS   INDIANA

90°   80°   70°

47

Map Grid Columns

A   B   C   D   E   F

50°

BRITISH COLUMBIA

ALBERTA

• Saskatoon

• Calgary

SASKATCHEWAN

Vancouver I.

• **Vancouver**

• Lethbridge

• Regina

• Brandon

45°

• **Seattle**

• Tacoma

• Spokane

Olympia

WASHINGTON

• Great Falls

NORTH DAKOTA

• **Portland**

▲ *Mt St. Helens*

• Helena

MONTANA

• Bismarck

• Salem

Missouri

• Eugene

• Billings

SOUTH DAKOTA

OREGON

SALMON RIVER MTS.

• Pierre

UNITED

• Boise

IDAHO

40°

Snake

STATES

WYOMING

OF

AMERICA

NEVADA

Great Salt Lake

• Ogden

NEBRASKA

• Reno

• Salt Lake City

• Cheyenne

• Carson City

Great Basin

• Provo

San Francisco

• **Sacramento**

COLORADO

• **Denver**

125°

• **Oakland**

UTAH

Mt. Elbert 4399 ▲

• Colorado Springs

KANS

• **San Jose**

SIERRA NEVADA

• Pueblo

35°

• Fresno

Mt. Whitney 4418 ▲

Las Vegas •

Colorado

Wic

CALIFORNIA

Death Valley

Grand Canyon

• Bakersfield

Colorado Plateau

• Santa Barbara

San Bernardino •

• Santa Fe

Oklahoma

• **Los Angeles**

ARIZONA

• Albuquerque

Amarillo •

OKLAH

• **Long Beach**

• **San Diego**

• **Phoenix**

NEW MEXICO

• Wichita Falls

• Tijuana

• Mexicali

30°

Fort W

• Tucson

Abilene •

PACIFIC OCEAN

TEXA

El Paso •

Ciudad Juárez

Austi

Hermosillo •

San Anton

Rio Grande

• Corpus Ch

25°

Gulf of California

• Chihuahua

Nuevo Laredo •

• Ciudad Obregón

Brown

MEXICO

Reynosa •

Saltillo •

■ **Monterr**

Scale

miles

0   200   400

0   200   400   600

kilometres

48

H   J   K   L   M   N   1

A D A   ONTARIO   QUEBEC   NEW BRUNSWICK   2

Fort Rupert

St. Lawrence

peg   Timmins   Quebec   Fredericton

Thunder Bay   Trois-Riviéres   MAINE   Saint John

Lake Superior   Montreal   Bangor

Sault Sainte Marie   Ottawa   Burlington   Augusta   3

MINNESOTA   MICHIGAN   Peterborough   Kingston   NEW YORK   VERMONT   NEW HAMPSHIRE

Minneapolis   Lake Huron   Toronto   Lake Ontario   Rochester   Utica   Albany   Worcester   Boston

St. Paul   WISCONSIN   Hamilton   Syracuse   Hartford   MASS.

Green Bay   London   Buffalo   Hudson   CONN.   R.I. Providence

x Falls   Madison   Grand Rapids   Lake Erie

ux City   IOWA   Milwaukee   Lansing   Detroit   Cleveland   PENNSYLVANIA   Newark   New York   4

Cedar Rapids   Lake Michigan   Youngstown   MTS.   N.J.   Philadelphia

Des Moines   Davenport   Chicago   Toledo   Akron   Pittsburgh   Altoona   DEL.

Omaha   Peoria   INDIANA   OHIO   Dayton   Columbus   Baltimore   MARYLAND

ILLINOIS   Decatur   Cincinnati   Charleston   Washington   D.C.

Kansas City   Springfield   Indianapolis   WEST VIRGINIA   VIRGINIA

eka   St. Louis   Evansville   Louisville   Richmond   Norfolk

MISSOURI   Ohio   Lexington   APPALACHIAN

sa   Springfield   KENTUCKY   Winston-   Greensboro

Fort Smith   Tennessee   Nashville   Salem   Raleigh   70°   ATLANTIC

ARKANSAS   TENNESSEE   Knoxville   Mt. Mitchell   NORTH CAROLINA   OCEAN   5

Memphis   2037   Charlotte

Chattanooga   SOUTH CAROLINA

Little Rock   Columbia

Birmingham   Atlanta   Augusta   Charleston

ARKANSAS   Tuscaloosa   ALABAMA   Columbus   Savannah

las   Monroe   MISSISSIPPI   Montgomery   GEORGIA

Shreveport   Jackson   Jacksonville

LOUISIANA   Baton Rouge   Mobile   Tallahassee   6

uston   Port Arthur   Pensacola   FLORIDA

New Orleans   Orlando

Galveston   Tampa

Gulf of Mexico   Fort Lauderdale

Miami   Nassau

BAHAMAS

Florida Keys   7

CUBA

95°   90°   85°   80°   75°

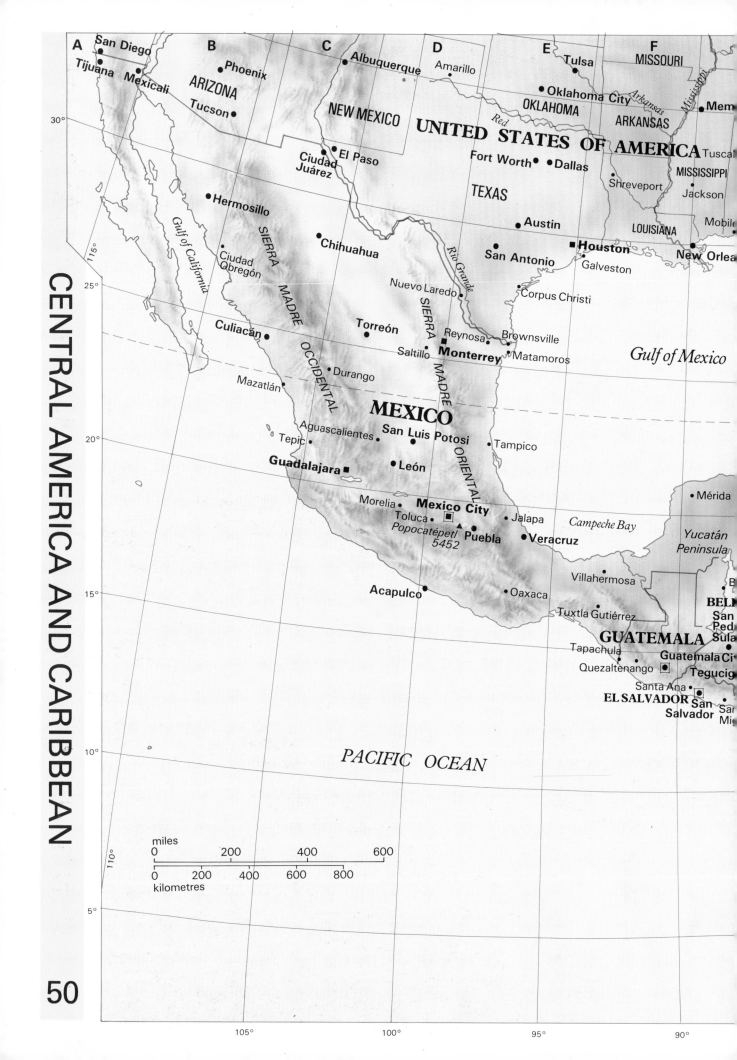

A B C D E F

San Diego
Tijuana
Mexicali
ARIZONA
Phoenix
Tucson

Albuquerque
Amarillo
NEW MEXICO
Tulsa
MISSOURI
Oklahoma City
OKLAHOMA
Arkansas
Mississippi
Mem

UNITED STATES OF AMERICA
Tusca

Ciudad Juárez
El Paso
Fort Worth
Dallas
Shreveport
MISSISSIPPI
Jackson

TEXAS
Austin
LOUISIANA
Mobile

30°

Hermosillo
Gulf of California
Ciudad Obregón

SIERRA

Chihuahua
Rio Grande
San Antonio
Houston
Galveston
New Orlea

25°

Nuevo Laredo
Corpus Christi

Culiacán
Torreón
SIERRA
Reynosa
Brownsville
Gulf of Mexico

MADRE
Saltillo
Monterrey
Matamoros

OCCIDENTAL
Durango
MADRE

Mazatlán

MEXICO

Aguascalientes
San Luis Potosi
ORIENTAL
Tampico

Tepic
León
20°

Guadalajara

Morelia
Mexico City
Mérida

Toluca
Jalapa
Campeche Bay

Popocatépetl
5452
Puebla
Veracruz
Yucatán Peninsula

Villahermosa

Acapulco
Oaxaca
15°

Tuxtla Gutiérrez
B

BEL
GUATEMALA
San
Ped
Sula

Tapachula
Guatemala Ci

Quezaltenango
Teguciga

Santa Ana
San
EL SALVADOR
San
Salvador
San
Mig

10°

PACIFIC OCEAN

miles
0   200   400   600

0   200   400   600   800
kilometres

5°

115°
110°
105°
100°
95°
90°

CENTRAL AMERICA AND CARIBBEAN

50

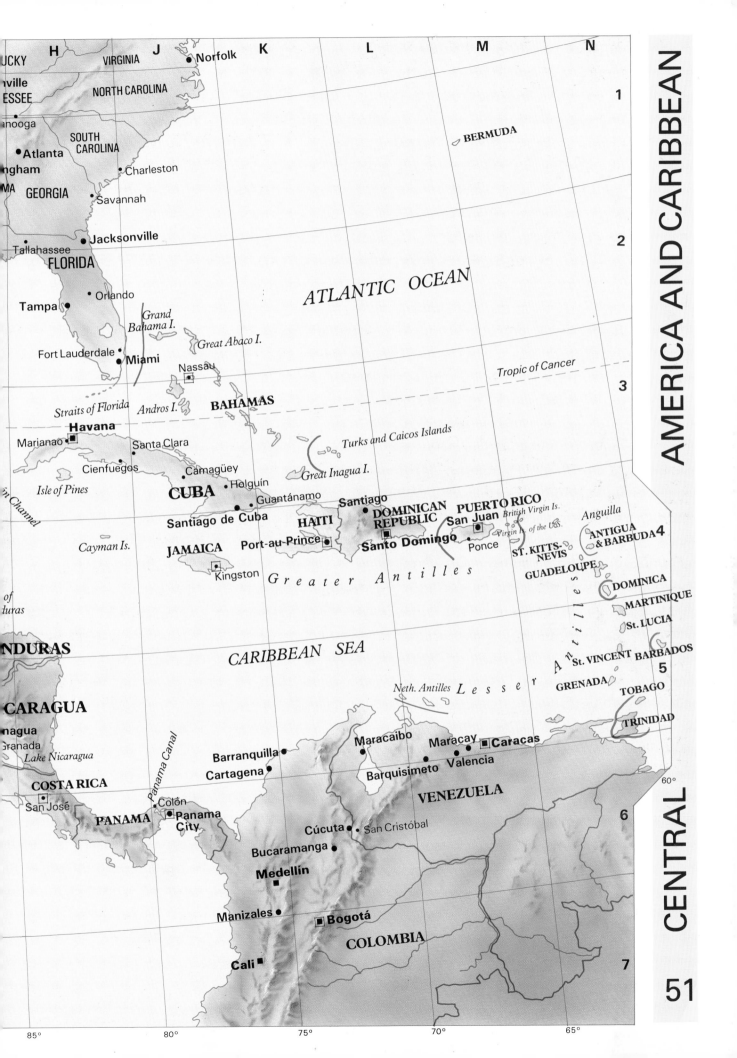

H J K L M N

1

VIRGINIA
UCKY
•Norfolk
ville
NORTH CAROLINA
ESSEE
nooga

BERMUDA

•Atlanta
SOUTH
CAROLINA
ngham
•Charleston
MA
GEORGIA
•Savannah

2

Tallahassee •Jacksonville
FLORIDA
•Orlando

ATLANTIC OCEAN

Tampa•
*Grand
Bahama I.*
Tropic of Cancer
Fort Lauderdale
Great Abaco I.
•Miami
Nassau

3

Straits of Florida *Andros I.* **BAHAMAS**

Havana
Marianao•
Santa Clara
Turks and Caicos Islands

Cienfuegos
Camagüey
Great Inagua I.
Isle of Pines
•Helguín
CUBA
Guantánamo
Santiago
DOMINICAN **PUERTO RICO**
British Virgin Is. *Anguilla*
Santiago de Cuba
REPUBLIC
San Juan
Virgin Is. of the US.
ANTIGUA
n Channel
HAITI
Santo Domingo
ST. KITTS- **& BARBUDA** 4
Cayman Is.
JAMAICA Port-au-Prince
Ponce
NEVIS
GUADELOUPE
Kingston
G r e a t e r   A n t i l l e s
DOMINICA
of
uras
MARTINIQUE
St. LUCIA

CARIBBEAN SEA
L e s s e r St. VINCENT **BARBADOS**

5
NDURAS
Neth. Antilles *A n t i l l e s* **GRENADA**
TOBAGO
CARAGUA
TRINIDAD
nagua
Maracaibo
Maracay **Caracas**
Granada
Lake Nicaragua
Barranquilla
Barquisimeto Valencia
Cartagena
VENEZUELA
60°
COSTA RICA
San José
Colón
PANAMA Panama
City
Cúcuta •San Cristóbal

6
Bucaramanga
Medellín
Manizales
Bogotá
COLOMBIA

Cali

7

85° 80° 75° 70° 65°

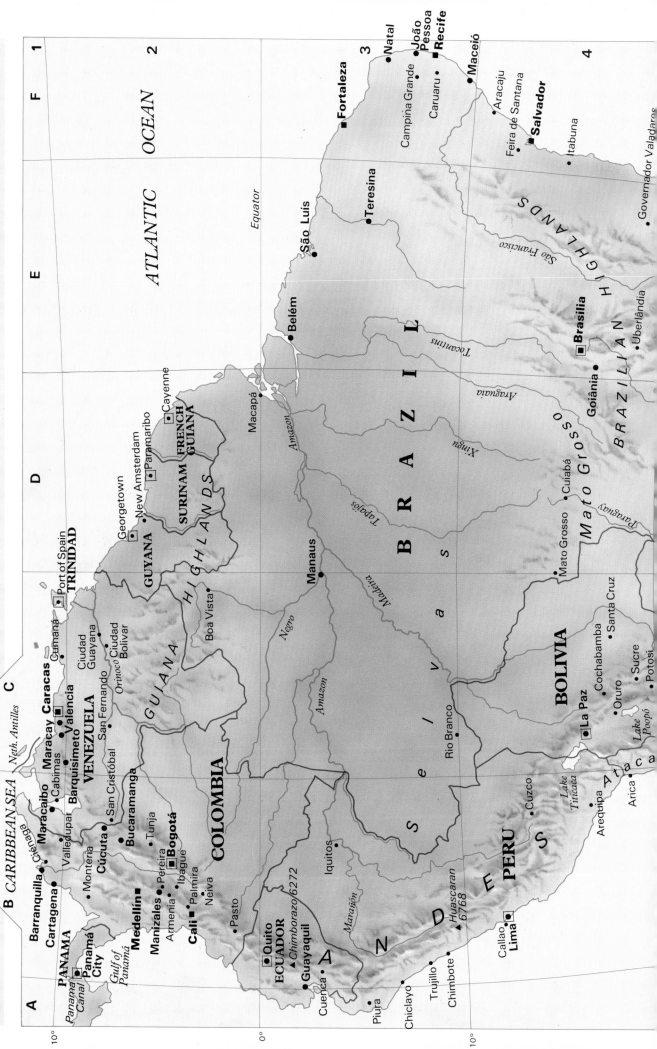

A   B   C   D   E   F

1

2

3

4

CARIBBEAN SEA

Neth. Antilles

ATLANTIC

OCEAN

Equator

PANAMA

Panama Canal

Panamá City

Gulf of Panamá

Barranquilla

Cartagena

Ciénaga

Maracaibo

Cabimas

Valledupar

Montería

Cúcuta

San Cristóbal

Bucaramanga

Tunja

VENEZUELA

Maracay Caracas

Valencia

Barquisimeto

Cumaná

Port of Spain

TRINIDAD

Georgetown

New Amsterdam

Paramaribo

Cayenne

GUYANA

SURINAM

FRENCH GUIANA

Ciudad Guayana

Ciudad Bolívar

San Fernando

Orinoco

G U I A N A

H I G H L A N D S

Boa Vista

Negro

Macapá

Amazon

Belém

São Luís

Teresina

Fortaleza

Natal

João Pessoa

Recife

Campina Grande

Caruaru

Maceió

Aracaju

Feira de Santana

Salvador

Itabuna

Governador Valadares

COLOMBIA

Medellín

Manizales

Armenia

Pereira

Ibagué

Bogotá

Palmira

Cali

Neiva

Pasto

Quito

ECUADOR

Chimborazo 6272

Guayaquil

Cuenca

Piura

Chiclayo

Trujillo

Chimbote

Iquitos

Marañón

Huascarán 6768

PERU

Callao

Lima

Cuzco

Arequipa

Arica

Atacama

A   N   D   E   S

Manaus

Amazon

Madeira

Rio Branco

S   e   l   v   a   s

BOLIVIA

La Paz

Cochabamba

Oruro

Poopó

Lake Poopó

Lake Titicaca

Sucre

Potosí

Santa Cruz

B   R   A   Z   I   L

Tapajós

Xingu

Tocantins

Araguaia

Paraguay

Mato Grosso

Mato Grosso

Cuiabá

Goiânia

Brasília

Uberlândia

BRAZILIAN

HIGHLANDS

São Francisco

10°

0°

10°

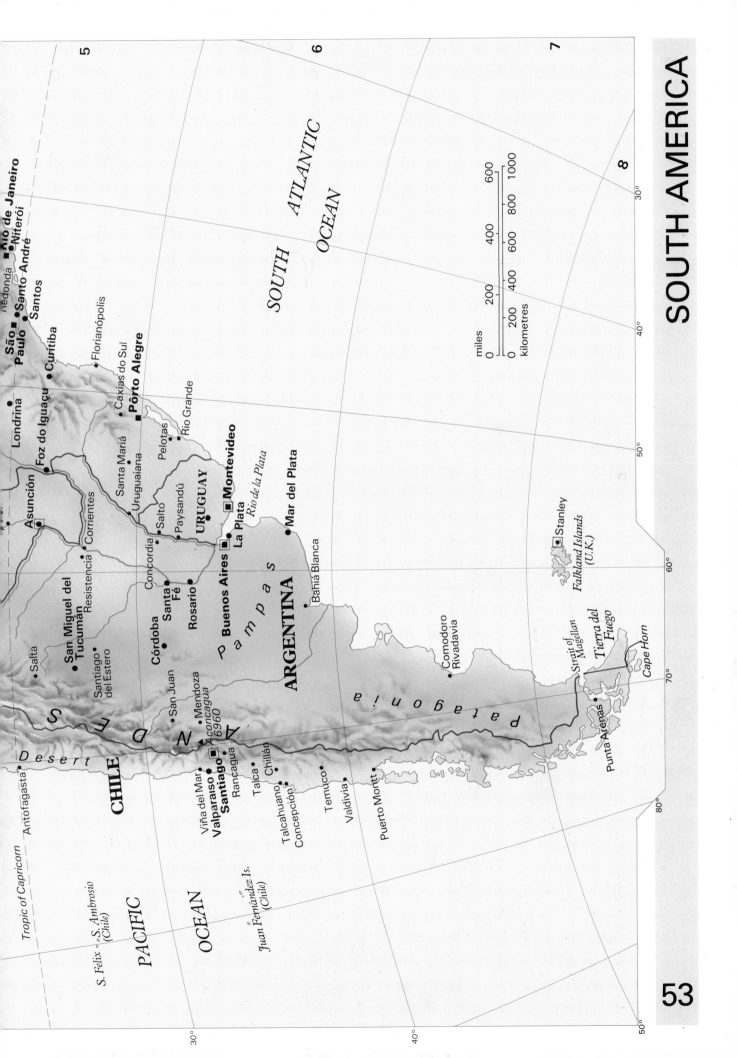

Rio de Janeiro
Niterói
Santo André
São Paulo
Santos
Curitiba
Londrina
Foz do Iguaçu
Florianópolis
Caxias do Sul
Pôrto Alegre
Rio Grande
Santa Mariá
Uruguaiana
Pelotas
Asunción
Corrientes
Resistencia
Concordia
Salto
Paysandú
URUGUAY
Montevideo
La Plata
Rio de la Plata
Salta
San Miguel del Tucumán
Santiago del Estero
Córdoba
Santa Fé
Rosario
P Buenos Aires
Mar del Plata
Bahiá Blanca
San Juan
Mendoza
Aconcagua 6960
ARGENTINA
P a m p a s
Antofagasta
Desert
S. Felix ● S. Ambrosio (Chile)
Tropic of Capricorn
CHILE
A N D E S
Viña del Mar
Valparaíso
Santiago
Rancagua
Talca
Talcahuano
Concepción
Chillán
Temuco
Valdivia
Puerto Montt
Juan Fernández Is. (Chile)
PACIFIC
OCEAN
P a t a g o n i a
Comodoro Rivadavia
Strait of Magellan
Tierra del Fuego
Cape Horn
Punta Arenas
Stanley
Falkland Islands (U.K.)
SOUTH
ATLANTIC
OCEAN

5
6
7
8

30°
40°
50°
60°
70°
80°

30°
40°
50°

miles
0   200   400   600
0   200   400   600   800   1000
kilometres

INDONESIA

Sumba

Timor

Melville I.

TIMOR SEA

•Darwin

ARNHEM LAND

Katherine

Groot
Eyl.

G

Birdum

•Wyndham

KIMBERLEY
PLATEAU

•Derby

Broome

Hall's Creek

BARKLY
TABLELAI

•Tennant Creek

Great Sandy Desert

NORTHERN TERRITORY

•Port Hedland

•Dampier

A U S T R A L I A

HAMERSLEY
RANGE

MACDONNELL RANGE

•Mount Newman

Tropic of Capricorn

•Alice Springs

BARLEE RANGE

Gibson Desert

Simpson
Desert

Carnarvon

▲Ayers Rock
867

MUSGRAVE RANGES

WESTERN AUSTRALIA

Lake E

•Mount Magnet

Great Victoria Desert

SOUTH AUSTRALIA

•Woomer

Geraldton

•Kalgoorlie

N u l l a r b o r   P l a i n

Eucla

Ceduna

Port Augus

•Moora

Coolgardie

Eyre Pen.

•Northam

Perth

Fremantle
Mandurah

•Narrogin

Esperance

Great Australian Bight

P
P

Bunbury

Port Lincoln

Adela

Augusta

Spencer Gulf

Albany

Kangaroo I.

INDIAN

OCEAN

miles
0   200   400

0   200   400   600
kilometres

115°   120°   125°   130°   135°

Cape York

**PAPUA
NEW GUINEA**

entaria

GREAT BARRIER REEF

Solomon
Islands

1

• Cooktown

2

• Normanton

• Cairns

CORAL   SEA

GREAT DIVIDING RANGE

unt Isa

• Hughenden

• Townsville • Bowen

3

• Mackay

• Winton

Great

• Barcaldine

QUEENSLAND

• Rockhampton

160°   165°

4

rtesian

• Bundaberg

N   O

Basin

• Charleville

• Maryborough

35°
• Kaitaia

• Whangarei

• Toowoomba

Brisbane

• Goondiwindi

*Gold
Coast*

5

Auckland

North I.

• Waihi

• Bourke

• Lismore

Hamilton •

• Tauranga
Rotorua •

9

R. Darling

• Narrabri

• Grafton

Waitara •

• Opotiki

• Nyngan

• Tamworth

Lake Taupo

• Taupo

• Broken Hill

Port Macquarie

New Plymouth •

Gisborne •

NEW SOUTH WALES

• Dubbo

• Taree

Mt Egmont ▲
2518

▲
2797

• Napier

• Orange

DIVIDING RANGE

Newcastle

6

Wanganui •

R. Murray

• Katoomba

Sydney

TASMAN

Levin •

• Palmerston North

Wagga Wagga •

• Wollongong

SEA

Nelson •

• Masterton
Cook Strait

VICTORIA

Canberra

40°

Blenheim •

◉**Wellington**

• Albury

G R E A T

155°

NEW ZEALAND

• Wangaratta

▲ *Mt Kosciusko*
2230

Westport •

South I.

10

• Bendigo
• Ballarat

Greymouth •

SOUTH

ount
ambier

Melbourne

7

SOUTHERN ALPS

Christchurch

PACIFIC

• Geelong • Morwell

M

Mt Cook
3764 ▲

OCEAN

rrnambool

• Timaru

King I. *Bass Strait* *Flinders I.*

• Wanaka

45°

• Devonport

• Alexandra

• Launceston

• Dunedin

Mt Ossa ▲
1617

TASMANIA

• Gore

• Hobart

8

Invercargill •

• Balclutha

miles
0   100   200   300

0   100 200 300 400
kilometres

11

Stewart I.

145°   150°

170°   175°

55

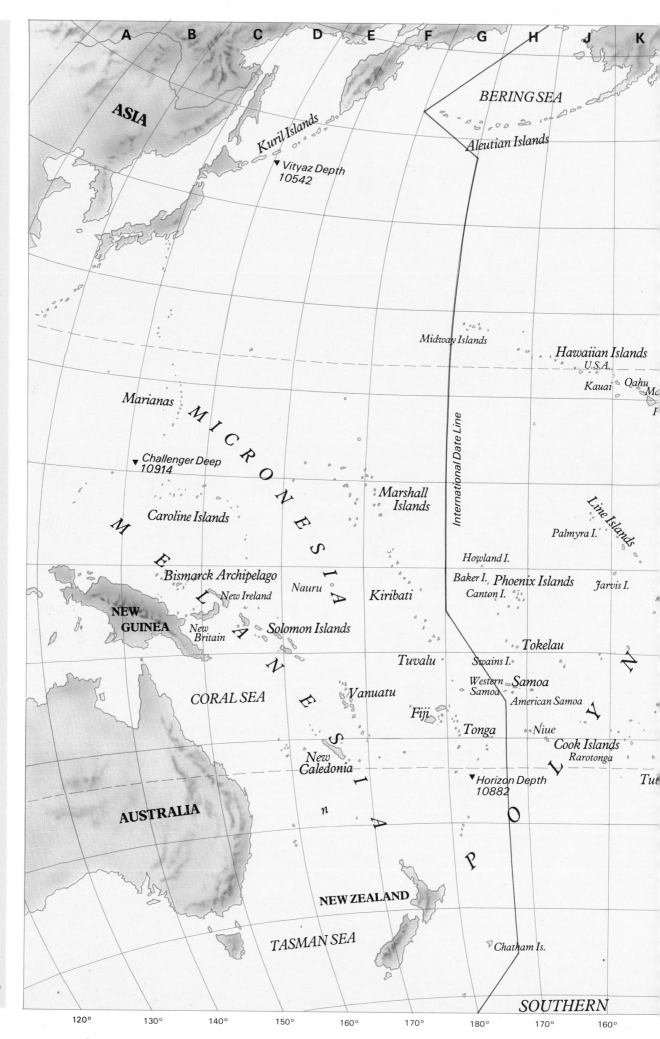

A B C D E F G H J K

ASIA

BERING SEA

Kuril Islands

Aleutian Islands

▼ Vityaz Depth
10542

Midway Islands

Hawaiian Islands
U.S.A.
Kauai Qahu Mo

MICRONESIA

Marianas

▼ Challenger Deep
10914

Marshall
Islands

Line Islands

Palmyra I.

Caroline Islands

MELANESIA

Howland I.

Baker I. Phoenix Islands
Canton I.

Jarvis I.

Bismarck Archipelago

Nauru

Kiribati

New Ireland

NEW
GUINEA
New
Britain
Solomon Islands

Tokelau

Tuvalu

Swains I.

Western
Samoa Samoa

Vanuatu

American Samoa

CORAL SEA

Fiji

Tonga

Niue

Cook Islands
Rarotonga

New
Caledonia

POLYNESIA

Tut

▼ Horizon Depth
10882

AUSTRALIA

n

NEW ZEALAND

TASMAN SEA

Chatham Is.

International Date Line

120° 130° 140° 150° 160° 170° 180° 170° 160°

SOUTHERN

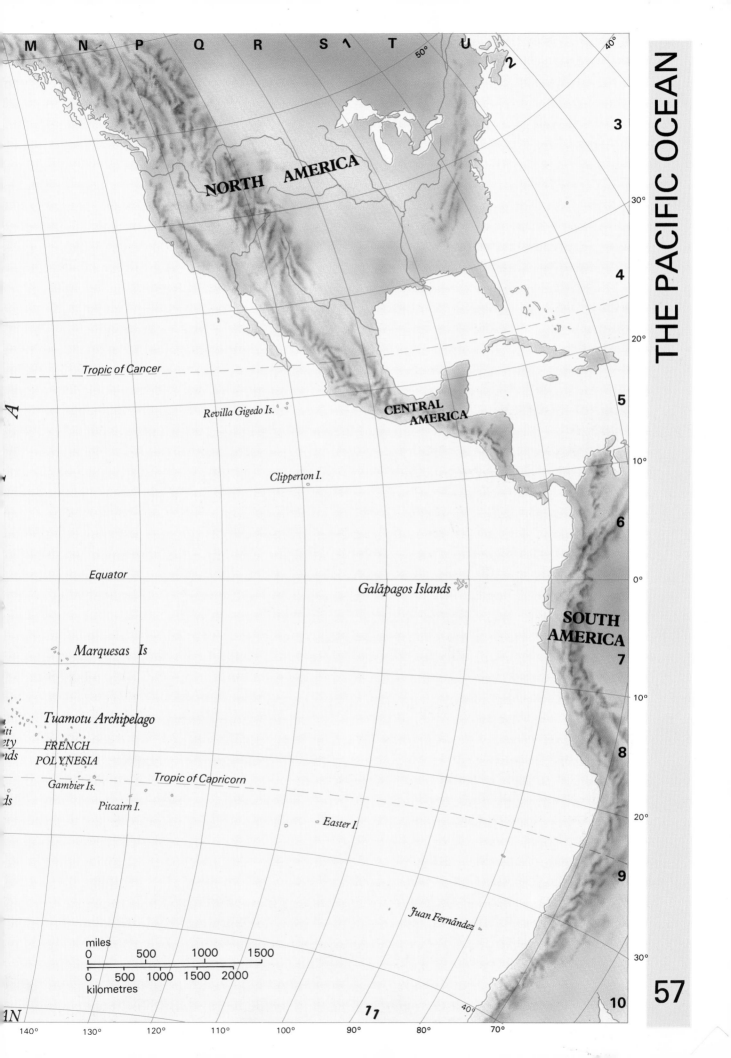

M N P Q R S ʌ T U

50°

40°

2

3

4

30°

20°

Tropic of Cancer

5

Revilla Gigedo Is.

10°

Clipperton I.

6

Equator

0°

Galápagos Islands

SOUTH
AMERICA

Marquesas Is

7

10°

Tuamotu Archipelago

FRENCH
POLYNESIA

8

Gambier Is.

Tropic of Capricorn

20°

Pitcairn I.

Easter I.

9

Juan Fernández

NORTH AMERICA

CENTRAL
AMERICA

A

30°

miles
0   500   1000   1500

0   500   1000   1500   2000
kilometres

10

1N

11

140°   130°   120°   110°   100°   90°   80°   70°   40°

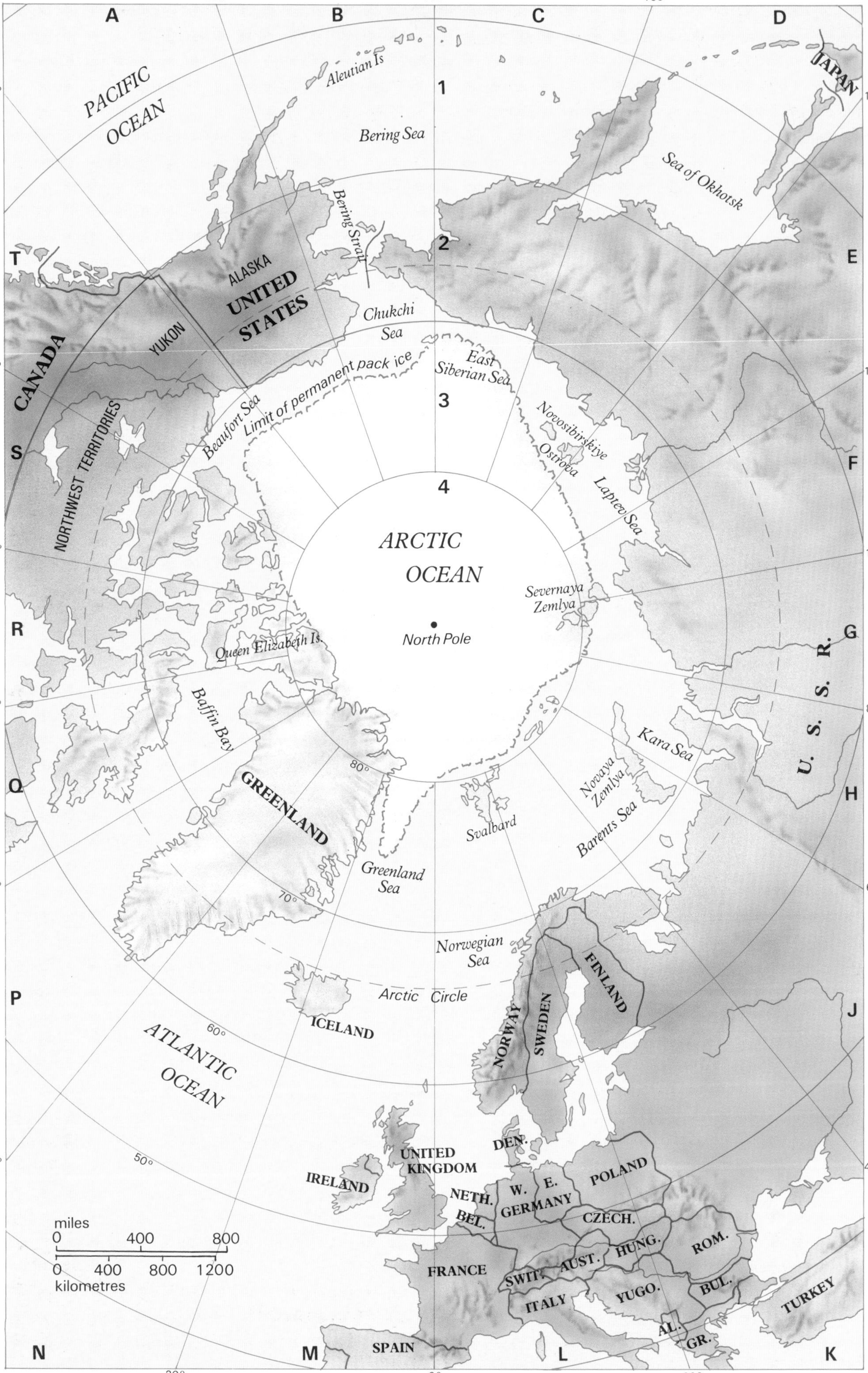

THE ARCTIC

A B 1 C D

160° 180° 160°

140°

PACIFIC OCEAN

Aleutian Is

Bering Sea

JAPAN

Sea of Okhotsk

2

T

ALASKA
UNITED
STATES

E

Bering Strait

Chukchi Sea

120°

CANADA

YUKON

Beaufort Sea

Limit of permanent pack ice

East Siberian Sea

Novosibirskiye Ostrova

Laptev Sea

3

S

NORTHWEST TERRITORIES

4

ARCTIC
OCEAN

F

100°

Severnaya Zemlya

R

Queen Elizabeth Is.

North Pole

U. S. S. R.

G

80°

Baffin Bay

80°

Kara Sea

Q

GREENLAND

Novaya Zemlya

H

Svalbard

Barents Sea

70°

Greenland Sea

60°

Norwegian Sea

NORWAY SWEDEN FINLAND

J

P

Arctic Circle

60°

ICELAND

50°

ATLANTIC
OCEAN

DEN.

40°

UNITED
KINGDOM

IRELAND

NETH.
BEL.

W. E.
GERMANY

POLAND

CZECH.

FRANCE

SWIT. AUST. HUNG.

ROM.

ITALY

YUGO.

BUL.

TURKEY

AL.
GR.

N M SPAIN L K

20° 0° 20°

miles
0   400   800

0   400   800   1200
kilometres

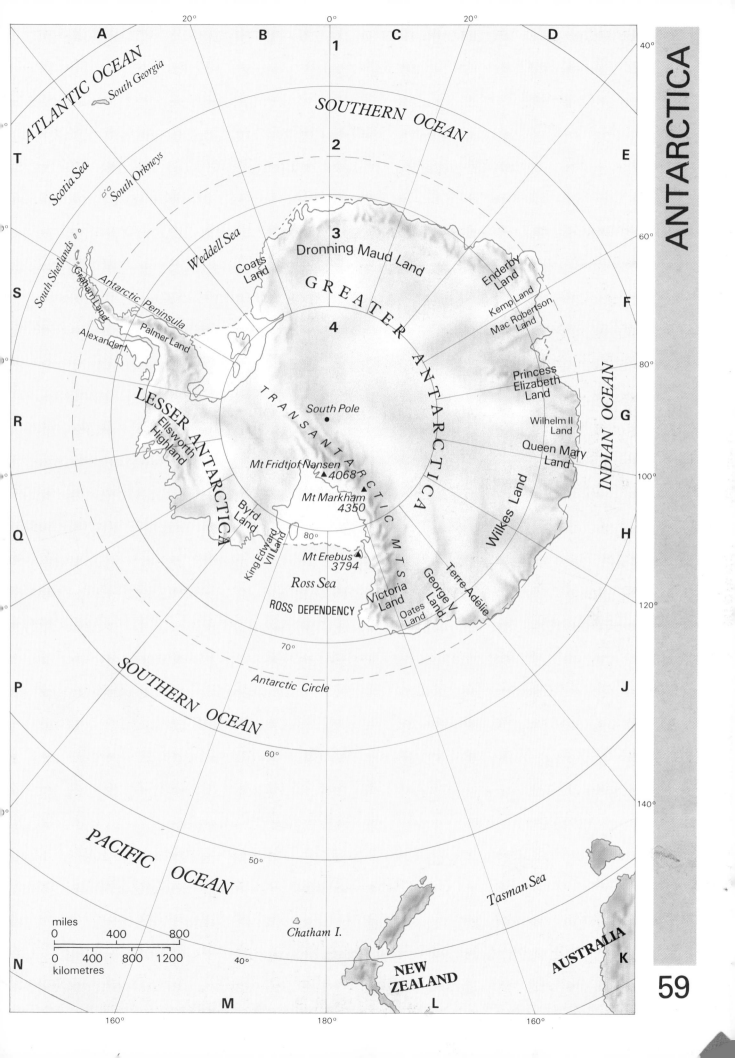

A

B

1

C

D

E

ATLANTIC OCEAN

South Georgia

SOUTHERN OCEAN

T

Scotia Sea

South Orkneys

2

South Shetlands

Weddell Sea

3

Dronning Maud Land

Enderby Land

Coats Land

G R E A T E R

Kemp Land

S

Graham Land

Antarctic Peninsula

Mac Robertson Land

Alexander I.

Palmer Land

4

A N T A R C T I C A

Princess Elizabeth Land

F

LESSER ANTARCTICA

T R A N S A N T A R C T I C

South Pole

Wilhelm II Land

INDIAN OCEAN

R

Ellsworth Highland

Queen Mary Land

G

Mt Fridtjof Nansen
▲4068

Byrd Land

Mt Markham
4350

Wilkes Land

Q

King Edward VII Land

80°

M T S

H

Mt Erebus ▲
3794

Terre Adélie

Ross Sea

George V Land

ROSS DEPENDENCY

Victoria Land

Oates Land

70°

P

SOUTHERN OCEAN

Antarctic Circle

J

60°

PACIFIC OCEAN

50°

140°

Tasman Sea

miles

0   400   800

Chatham I.

0   400   800   1200

kilometres

N

40°

NEW ZEALAND

AUSTRALIA

K

160°

M

180°

L

160°

FLAGS

FLAGS

On the following pages the national flags of the countries of the world are shown as they stand as we go to press. As governments change, so do the flags of countries. As you look through the pages you will find there are common features that link countries of similar background, culture and religion. Commonwealth countries sometimes retain a link with the United Kingdom in their flags. In the Arab world the Pan-Arab colours of red, white, black and green will be found, while red, yellow and green are the Pan-African colours often found in that Continent. The red flag and the Communist star are used by the Soviet Union and some other Communist states, whereas flags with crosses have characterised Christian countries, and flags with crescents and stars Muslim ones.

Flags of the Americas

United States

Before the start of the War of Independence in 1775, a flag was flown by the Sons of Liberty with nine alternating red and white stripes, standing for the nine colonies that were in revolt against the British. In December of that year the Continental Colours were introduced, with 13 red and white stripes (for the colonies) and the British Union Flag in the canton. In 1777, 13 stars replaced the Union Flag. In 1795 the number of stars and stripes was increased to 15 and the flag became known as the

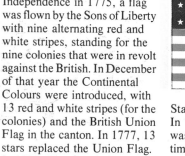

Star-spangled Banner (above). In 1818 the number of stripes was reduced to 13 and from that time each new state had its own star. The number was most recently increased in 1960 when Hawaii was admitted.

1 Alabama	13 Illinois	27 Nebraska	39 Rhode Island
2 Alaska	14 Indiana	28 Nevada	40 South
3 Arizona	15 Iowa	29 New	Carolina
4 Arkansas	16 Kansas	Hampshire	41 South Dakota
5 California	17 Kentucky	30 New Jersey	42 Tennessee
6 Colorado	18 Louisiana	31 New Mexico	43 Texas
7 Connecticut	19 Maine	32 New York	44 Utah
8 Delaware	20 Maryland	33 North	45 Vermont
* District of	21 Massachusetts	Carolina	46 Virginia
Columbia	22 Michigan	34 North Dakota	47 Washington
9 Florida	23 Minnesota	35 Ohio	48 West Virginia
10 Georgia	24 Mississippi	36 Oklahoma	49 Wisconsin
11 Hawaii	25 Missouri	37 Oregon	50 Wyoming
12 Idaho	26 Montana	38 Pennsylvania	* No number

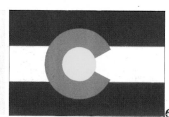

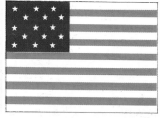

17

18

19

20

21

22

23

24

25

26 **MONTANA**

27

28 BATTLE BORN

29

30

31

32

33 MAY 20th 1775 · N ★ C · APRIL 12th 1776

34 NORTH DAKOTA

35

36 OKLAHOMA

37 STATE OF OREGON 1859

38

39 HOPE

40

41 SOUTH DAKOTA THE SUNSHINE STATE

42

43

44 1896

45

46

47

48

49 WISCONSIN 1848

50

Areas and population figures for countries are given in alphabetical order within groups.

COUNTRY	AREA Km²	POPULATION
NORTH AMERICA		
Canada	9,976,139	25,600,000
United States of America	9,363,123	239,280,000

Canada

The Red Ensign was used from 1892, with the arms in the fly until 1921 when they were replaced with a new shield. Attempts were made to find a more acceptable design, but it was not until 1965 that the present flag was adopted with the maple leaf emblem.

The twelve provinces and territories each have their own flag (adoption dates are shown in brackets):

Alberta (1968)

British Columbia (1960)

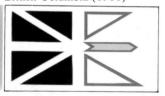

Newfoundland (1979)

Nova Scotia (1929)

Manitoba (1966)

New Brunswick (1965)

North-West Territories (1969)

Prince Edward Island (1964)

Ontario (1965)

Quebec (1948)

Saskatchewan (1969)

The Yukon (1968)

Flags of Central America

Mexico

The present flag was adopted in 1968. The emblem depicts the legendary founding of Mexico City. It shows an eagle, snake and cactus. The colours date back to 1821.

Guatemala

The colours of Central America are used vertically. The present simple design dates from 1871. The state flag shows the national bird of Guatemala, the quetzal, with its long tail feathers. It is a symbol of liberty.

Belize

On full independence from Britain in 1981, Belize added two red stripes to the flag. The coat of arms shows two men, the tools of the country's logging industry and the Latin motto 'I flourish in the shade'.

Honduras

The five stars stand for the original members of the United Provinces of Central America. The flag was officially adopted in 1949.

El Salvador

The traditional Central American colours were adopted in 1912. This flag is for use on land, while one bearing the national motto 'God, Union, Liberty' is used at sea.

Nicaragua

Without the national emblem, Nicaragua's flag is identical to that of the United Provinces of Central America, to which it once belonged. The present form dates from 1908.

Costa Rica

As one of the five states of the United Provinces of Central America, the flag (dating from 1848) retains the blue/white/blue sequence with an additional red stripe.

Panama

The flag dates from Panama's break with Colombia in 1903. Blue is for the Conservatives, red for the Liberals, white for the hope of peace. The red star stands for law and order, the blue star for public honesty.

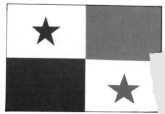

Flags of South America

Ecuador
Linked until 1830 with Colombia and Venezuela, Ecuador shares with them the flag designed by Francisco de Miranda, under which Simon Bolivar's armies marched.

Colombia
The colours of the flag (see above) represent the nation (yellow), separated by the sea (blue) from Spain whose tyranny the people would resist with their blood (red).

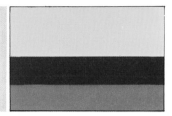

Venezuela
The flag was first used in 1806 when Miranda invaded (see Ecuador). The stars stand for the seven provinces. Only the state flag bears the coat of arms; the flag for civil use bears only the arc of seven stars.

Guyana
This design was adopted in 1966 on independence. The colours stand for the forests (green), the future (gold), the people's energy (red), their perseverance (black) and the rivers (white).

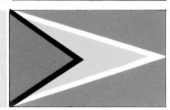

Surinam
The flag of Surinam, adopted on independence from the Netherlands in 1975, is based on that of the main political parties. The yellow star stands for unity and the nation's golden future.

French Guiana
A French possession since 1676, French Guiana is now an overseas department of France. Treated as if it were part of the mainland, its citizens elect members to the French parliament. The flag is the French tricolour.

Peru
General José de San Martin led the liberation of Peru from Spanish rule in 1820 and is said to have chosen red and white as the national colours after a flock of flamingoes flew over his troops.

Brazil
The motto 'Order and Progress' is inscribed on the central sphere. The 23 stars, representing the states and Federal District, are arranged in the pattern of the sky at night as it is seen over Brazil.

Paraguay
The only national flag with a different design on each side. The State Emblem, shown here, bears the gold star of May, representing liberation from Spain. The reverse side displays the Treasury Seal.

Bolivia
The colours date from the liberation of 1825. The red stands for the army's valour, yellow for the nation's rich mineral resources, and green for the agricultural wealth of the country.

Uruguay
Flown since 1820 shortly after independence, the blue and white stripes and gold sun are derived from the flag and emblem of Argentina. The original nine provinces are represented in the nine stripes.

Chile
Inspired by the Stars and Stripes of the USA and adopted in the independence struggle in 1817, the white is for the snow on the Andes, blue for the sky and red for the blood of the patriots who died for their country.

Argentina
Blue and white were the colours used in the fight for freedom from Spain. The first flag was raised in 1812.

Falkland Islands
This British Dependent Territory flies the Blue Ensign. The sheep on the badge represents the islands' economic mainstay and the ship is the *Desire*, which sailed to discover the islands.

COUNTRY	AREA Km²	POPULATION
CENTRAL AMERICA		
Belize	22,963	166,200
Costa Rica	51,100	2,660,000
El Salvador	21,393	5,480,000
Guatemala	108,889	8,400,000
Honduras	112,088	4,370,000
Mexico	1,958,201	81,320,000
Nicaragua	130,000	3,160,000
Panama	78,046	2,180,000

COUNTRY	AREA Km²	POPULATION
SOUTH AMERICA		
Argentina	2,776,889	31,060,000
Bolivia	1,098,581	6,430,000
Brazil	8,511,965	138,000,000
Chile	756,945	12,070,000
Colombia	1,138,914	28,620,000
Ecuador	283,561	9,380,000
Falkland Islands	12,173	1,919
French Guiana	91,000	73,022
Guyana	214,970	950,000
Paraguay	409,752	3,680,000
Peru	1,285,216	19,700,000
Surinam	163,820	370,000
Uruguay	186,926	2,950,000
Venezuela	912,050	17,320,000

Flags of the Caribbean

Puerto Rico
A Commonwealth of the United States, the flag is only flown with the Stars and Stripes. The country fought with Cuba for independence from Spain and their flags are almost identical.

Cuba
The 'Lone Star' banner, dating from 1849, was not officially adopted until independence in 1902. The red triangle stands for freedom.

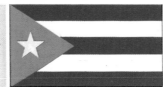

Haiti
The flag of Haiti is derived from that of France, to which it once belonged. The present design, first used in 1803, was restored in 1986.

Dominican Republic
Once a part of Haiti, the Republic's first flag was a white cross over the blue and red 'French' flag of Haiti. The quarters were rearranged into the present pattern in 1844.

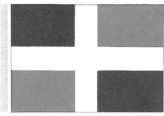

Bahamas
Adopted in 1973, the blue is for the sea that surrounds the 700 islands, the yellow the sands and the black the strength and unity of the people.

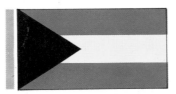

Turks and Caicos Islands
This British Territory flies the Blue Ensign with the coat of arms containing a conch shell, a spiny lobster and a turk's head cactus.

Montserrat
The shield of the Blue Ensign of this British colony dates back to 1909. The Passion cross is held by a female figure in green with a harp.

Cayman Islands
The Blue Ensign is flown by this British Dependent Territory, with the coat of arms, granted in 1958. It shows a turtle and a pineapple.

Bermuda
The Red Ensign with the coat of arms dates from 1915. A red lion holds the wreck of the *Sea Venture* – on which the first settlers sailed in 1609.

British Virgin Islands
A British Dependent Territory, the Blue Ensign carries the islands' badge. It shows a virgin with 12 oil lamps from the Bible story.

Virgin Islands of the United States
The flag of this American Dependency has been flown since 1921. It shows the American eagle with a shield between the letters 'V' and 'I'.

St Christopher-Nevis
Also known as St Kitts-Nevis, these two islands became an independent state in 1983 and hoisted a flag designed by a local art student. The two stars stand for hope and liberty.

Anguilla
Adopted in 1967, the white stands for peace, the blue stripe for hope and youthfulness, the dolphins for strength.

Dominica
On independence, Dominica adopted a flag featuring the parrot which also appears on the coat of arms, and the stars to represent the island's parishes.

Jamaica
Adopted on independence in 1962, the gold stands for the natural resources and sun, green for agriculture and the future, and black for hardships.

St Lucia
The symbol represents the two volcanic formations that rise up from the sea. The island is a former Associated State of Great Britain.

COUNTRY	AREA Km²	POPULATION
CARIBBEAN		
Anguilla	96	7,000
Antigua-Barbuda	442	81,500
Bahamas	13,939	230,000
Barbados	430	253,055
Bermuda	54	57,145
Cayman Islands	260	20,300
Cuba	114,524	10,150,000
Dominica	751	80,000
Dominican Republic	48,442	6,600,000
Grenada	344	115,000
Haiti	27,750	5,300,000
Jamaica	11,425	2,300,000
Montserrat	102	12,000
Netherlands Antilles	800	260,000
Puerto Rico	8,897	3,270,000
St Christopher-Nevis	262	43,309
St Lucia	616	136,952
St Vincent and the Grenadines	388	127,883
Trinidad and Tobago	5,130	1,200,000
Turks and Caicos Islands	430	7,436
British Virgin Islands	130	12,034
Virgin Islands of the United States	344	100,000

Antigua-Barbuda
Adopted in 1967, the flag was retained when the former Associated State of the United Kingdom gained independence in 1981.

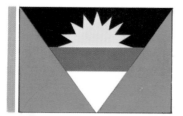

St Vincent and the Grenadines
On independence, St Vincent adopted a tricolour of blue, yellow and green, with its arms in the centre, but in 1985 these were replaced with three green diamonds.

Barbados
The truncated trident head comes from the pre-independence colonial badge. Adopted in 1966, the colours stand for the island's blue sea, blue sky and golden beaches.

Grenada
Adopted on independence in 1974, the flag illustrates the nutmeg, the main product. The stars stand for the seven parishes of the island. The colours stand for the sun, agriculture and the friendly people.

Netherlands-Antilles
The five stars stand for the five parts of this self-governing Dutch dependency. The colours recall those of the Dutch flag. Prior to 1986 there were six stars on the flag: Aruba became a separate dependency in 1986 and has its own flag.

Trinidad and Tobago
Adopted on independence in 1962, the red stands for the people's warmth and vitality, black for its strength and the islands' wealth, white for the sea and the people's hopes.

Flags of Africa

Egypt
Since 1958 Egypt has employed a flag of red, white and black but with a succession of different emblems in the centre. The present design, introduced in 1984, has the national arms in the centre.

Libya
The Libyan Arab Republic flew the flag of the Federation of Arab Republics until 1977 when it left the Federation. The plain green represents the nation's hope for a green revolution in agriculture.

Algeria
The flag, with its traditional Islamic symbol and colours, has flown since independence in 1962. It appeared in 1928 during the independence struggles, but the design may have been based on a far earlier patriotic flag.

Tunisia
The traditional symbols of the Muslim religion – the star and crescent – are in the centre of the flag which dates from the early 19th century. It was officially adopted on independence in 1956.

Morocco
The red flag was used for three centuries before the green Seal of Solomon was added in 1915. Morocco achieved independence in 1956.

COUNTRY	AREA Km²	POPULATION
AFRICA		
Algeria	2,381,741	22,600,000
Angola	1,246,700	8,960,000
Benin	112,622	4,142,000
Botswana	600,372	1,050,000
Burkina Faso	274,122	7,920,000
Burundi	27,834	4,920,000
Cameroon	475,442	9,880,000
Cape Verde	4,033	319,000
Central African Republic	622,983	2,700,000
Chad	1,284,000	5,120,000
Comoro Islands	2,171	430,000
Congo	342,000	1,980,000
Djibouti	23,200	297,000
Egypt	1,002,000	48,850,000
Equatorial Guinea	28,051	375,000
Ethiopia	1,221,900	42,000,000
Gabon	267,667	1,340,000
Gambia	11,295	687,817
Ghana	238,537	13,150,000
Guinea	245,857	6,410,000
Guinea-Bissau	36,125	875,000
Ivory Coast	322,463	10,600,000
Kenya	582,600	20,330,000
Lesotho	30,355	1,470,000
Liberia	111,369	2,190,000
Libya	1,759,540	3,960,000
Malagasy Republic (Madagascar)	587,044	8,000,000
Malawi	118,484	7,100,000
Mali	1,240,142	8,300,000
Mauritania	1,030,700	1,870,000
Mauritius	2,046	1,000,432
Morocco	458,730	21,160,000
Mozambique	801,589	14,140,000
Niger	1,267,000	6,600,000
Nigeria	923,768	116,200,000
Rwanda	26,338	6,320,000
St Helena	122	6,000
São Tomé and Principé	1,001	109,000
Senegal	196,192	6,700,000
Seychelles	308	65,244
Sierra Leone	73,326	3,520,000
Somalia (Somali Republic)	637,658	5,980,000
South Africa	1,123,226	23,380,000
Sudan	2,505,813	20,560,000
Swaziland	17,400	676,049
Tanzania	945,087	21,730,000
Togo	56,785	3,090,000
Tunisia	154,530	7,320,000
Uganda	236,860	13,990,000
Zaïre	2,344,885	34,250,000
Zambia	752,614	6,650,000
Zimbabwe	390,308	8,420,000

Sudan

Based on the post 1918 Arab revolt flag, this design has been flown since 1969. Added to the Pan-Arab colours is an Islamic green triangle to symbolise material prosperity and spiritual wealth.

Ethiopia

The tricolour was first flown as three separate pennants, one above the other. The combination of red, yellow and green dates from the late nineteenth century and appeared in flag form in 1897.

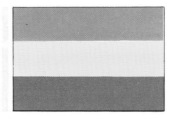

Djibouti

Djibouti (formerly Afars and Issas) gained independence from France in 1977. Its flag has two horizontal stripes, a white triangle in the hoist, with a five-pointed red star. It has been in use since 1972 when it symbolised the wish for independence.

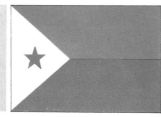

Somalia (Somali Republic)

British Somaliland (in the north) united with Somalia (in the south) in 1960 to form today's Somalia. The simple flag of the southern region of the country was adopted by the new country.

Kenya

Based on the flag of the Kenya African National Union which led the independence struggle, the design was adopted in 1963. The Masai warrior's shield and two crossed spears stand for defence of freedom.

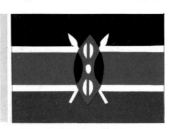

Uganda

The colours of the Uganda People's Congress were used for the national flag when the country gained independence in 1962. They represented the people (black), the sun (yellow), and brotherhood (red). A crested crane stands in the centre.

Tanzania

Tanganyika joined with Zanzibar to form Tanzania in 1964. The new flag has parts of the old flags of the two countries.

Rwanda

The tricolour of Pan-African colours adopted on independence in 1962 has an 'R' in the centre to distinguish it from the flag of Guinea.

Burundi

Introduced at the start of the Republic in 1966, the stars symbolise the nation's motto 'Unity, Work, Progress'. The colours represent peace (white), hope (green) and the struggle for independence (red).

Mauritania

Adopted in 1959 just before independence from France in 1960, the star and crescent reflect the Muslim religion followed by the majority. The country's official name is the Mauritanian Islamic Republic.

Mali

A French colony (French Sudan) until 1960, the Pan-African colours, used by the African Democratic Rally before independence, were arranged in the form of the French tricolour.

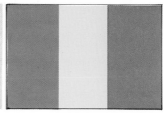

Senegal

Apart from the green five-pointed star which represents the people's Islamic faith, the flag is identical to Mali's. It was adopted in 1960 when the country gained its independence from France.

The Gambia

This former British colony, locked within Senegal, follows the course of the Gambia River. The flag, adopted in 1965, shows the blue river flowing through the green land with the sun overhead.

Guinea-Bissau

Adopted on independence from Portugal in 1973, the flag had been used since 1961 by the liberation movement. The colours are Pan-African.

Guinea

A former French colony, the design of the Republic's flag is based on the French tricolour, but using the Pan-African colours – red (for work), yellow (justice) and green (solidarity).

Sierra Leone

The colours of the flag that was adopted on independence from Britain in 1961 are derived from the coat of arms. Green stands for agriculture, white for peace and blue for the Atlantic Ocean which washes its shores.

Liberia

Founded in the early 19th century for freed black slaves from America, the flag adopted in 1847 was based on the Stars and Stripes, but has eleven stripes and a single white five-pointed star.

Ivory Coast

Like Guinea, Senegal, Mali and Cameroon, this former French colony adopted a flag based on the vertical stripes of the French tricolour on independence in 1959.

Burkina Faso

Formerly Upper Volta, this country adopted a new name and a new flag in 1984. The colours of the new flag are like those of the other West African countries.

Ghana

The colours, first hoisted by Ethiopia in 1894, were adopted by other former colonies as a sign of Pan-African unity after Ghana took the lead on independence in 1957.

Togo

The Togo Republic, which gained independence in 1960, flies the Pan-African colours – green stands for agriculture, yellow for mineral wealth and red for bloodshed. The white star stands for national purity.

Benin

In 1975 Benin became a People's Republic. The new flag is green with a red star in the upper hoist. The old Dahomey flag sported the red, yellow and green Pan-African colours.

Nigeria

The design was selected ahead of Nigeria's independence from Britain in 1960. The green stands for the country's forests and white is for peace.

Niger

Adopted in 1959 before independence from France in 1960, the orange disc in the centre represents the sun, the orange stripe the Sahara desert in the north, the white stands for goodness and purity, and the green for the grass of the south.

Cape Verde Islands

Formerly a Portuguese colony, the Pan-African flag was adopted in 1975. The emblem's five-pointed black star is above a garland of maize sheaves, two corn cobs and a clamshell.

Chad

Adopted in 1959, the colours are a compromise between those of France and Africa. Blue represents the sky, streams and hope, yellow the sun and desert, red the national sacrifice.

Cameroon

The Cameroons were formerly administered by Britain and France. When the French Cameroons became independent in 1960 the tricolour was adopted. Two stars were added when the British joined in 1961, to be replaced in 1975 by a single star.

Central African Republic

The flag was adopted when the country gained independence from France in 1960. It combines African and French colours to show the need for friendship.

Equatorial Guinea

Adopted in 1968, green is for the natural resources and wealth of the land, blue is for the sea, white is for peace and and red for the nation's struggle for independence.

São Tomé and Principe

These two islands gained independence from Portugal in 1975. The five-pointed stars in the tricolour stand for the two islands.

Gabon

Adopted on independence from France in 1960, the green stands for the country's forests and lumber industry, the blue for the sea, and the yellow for the sun.

Congo

Independence was achieved in 1960 and ten years later the People's Republic was created, with a new red flag and emblem. The colours are the Pan-African colours – red, yellow and green. A hammer and hoe (rather than a sickle) represent industry and agriculture.

Zaïre

The Pan-African colours were adopted by Zaïre in 1971. The arm in the centre, originally the Popular Movement's emblem, holds a blazing torch – as a reminder of the spirit of revolution and the lives of dead revolutionaries.

St Helena

The flag of this British dependency, situated off the west coast of Africa, comprises the Blue Ensign with the shield taken from the coat of arms.

Angola

The flag is based on that of the Popular Movement for the Liberation of Angola during the country's struggle for independence which came in 1975. The half gear wheel and machete are reminiscent of the Soviet hammer and sickle.

Zambia

Adopted on independence in 1964, the eagle stands for freedom. The colours are those of the party that led the independence struggle.

Malawi

The colours of the flag were used by the Malawi Congress Party and when the country became independent in 1964 they were adopted for the national flag. The rising sun was added to indicate a new era.

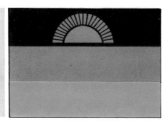

Botswana

When the country became independent in 1966, the markings of the zebra were chosen to express the equality of black and white people. Blue represents the nation's most vital need – rainwater.

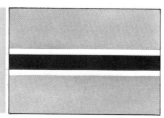

Zimbabwe

Adopted after legal independence in 1980, the new flag includes colours from the independence movements' flags and a white triangle for the minority population with the soapstone bird emblem.

Mozambique

Mozambique adopted a new flag in 1983, but it is still in the colours of the movement which took the country to independence in 1975. The book, hoe and rifle also appear in the coat of arms.

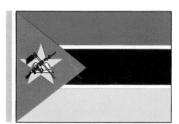

South Africa

Since 1928 South Africa has flown a flag that has its origins with the first Dutch settlers. On the central stripe are the Union Flag, the flag of the old Orange Free State, and the flag of the Transvaal.

Lesotho

The emblem of the flag of Lesotho is a simplified version of the coat of arms: a shield, a knobkerrie and an ostrich feather sceptre. The colours stand for peace, rain and plenty – the words of the national motto.

Swaziland

Flown since independence in 1968, the flag is based on that of the Swazi Pioneer Corps. The emblem has the weapons of a warrior – the ox-hide shield, two assegai (throwing spears) and a fighting stick.

Comoro Islands

The flag flown since independence from France in 1975 reflects the islanders' Muslim faith. The stars represent the four islands, although Mayotte remains a French Dependency.

Seychelles

A new flag was adopted in 1977. The wavy design is said to suggest the Indian Ocean in which the Seychelles Islands lie.

Democratic Republic of Madagascar (Republic of Malagasy)

Madagascar's people came from South-East Asia and brought the historic red and white colours with them. The present flag was adopted in 1958 when the country first became a Republic.

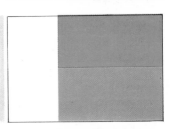

Mauritius

The flag of this small island, east of Madagascar, was adopted on independence in 1968. Red is for the people's struggle and bloodshed, blue for the Indian Ocean, yellow for the bright future and green for the vegetation.

Flags of Oceania

Fiji
Independent since 1970, Fiji retains the British Ensign. Its own coat of arms shows a British lion, sugar cane, a coconut palm, bananas and a dove of peace.

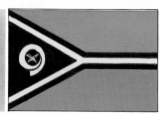

Vanuatu
On independence from both Britain and France in 1980, Vanuatu (formerly New Hebrides) adopted an original design which has a boar's horn in the triangle in the hoist.

Tonga
The flag was adopted in 1875 on the understanding that it would never be changed. Symbolising the islanders' Christianity, it was retained on independence.

Nauru
The flag shows this tiny island's position just south of the Equator. The 12 points of the star represent the 12 tribes of Nauru.

Kiribati
Since 1979 the flag has consisted solely of the coat of arms. It shows a frigate bird flying over the sun as it rises over the Pacific Ocean.

Tuvalu
Formerly the Ellice Islands, Tuvalu's flag retains the Union flag and shows the position of the nine main islands in the group.

Solomon Islands
Adopted on independence in 1978, the flag has a star for each island on a blue (sea) and green (land) field, with a yellow (sun) stripe.

Western Samoa
The flag returns to the red and white of the pre-colonial flags of the kingdom of Samoa. The stars represent the Southern Cross constellation.

Australia
The national flag has the Union flag showing the link with Great Britain, the stars of the Southern Cross constellation and the seven-pointed Commonwealth Star – one point for each of the original States and one for the Dependent Territories. The predominately blue and white flag also echoes the banner of the Eureka Stockade gold miners against government corruption and oppression in the nineteenth century.

The States have the Blue Ensign with their own badges:

New South Wales – St George's Cross with a lion and four eight-pointed stars;

Queensland – blue Maltese Cross with royal crown;

South Australia – white-backed piping shrike (the Murray magpie);

Tasmania – red lion;

Victoria – a crown over the Southern Cross;

Western Australia – black swan on a yellow field;

Northern Territory – achieving self-government in 1978, the Northern Territory adopted a distinctive flag with the Southern Cross and a desert rose on an ochre background.

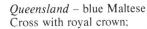

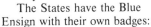

COUNTRY	AREA Km²	POPULATION
OCEANIA		
American Samoa	197	32,400
Australia	7,682,300	15,451,900
Cook Islands	234	20,000
Federated States of Micronesia	1,800	102,000
Fiji	18,333	714,000
Guam	541	120,000
Kiribati	717	60,000
Nauru	21	8,042
New Zealand	268,704	3,300,000
Niue	259	4,000
Northern Marianas	479	14,000
Papua New Guinea	462,840	3,420,000
Solomon Islands	28,446	270,000
Tonga	748	105,000
Tuvalu	25	8,229
Vanuatu	14,763	135,000
Western Samoa	2,841	162,000

New Zealand
The flag was designed in 1869 and retained on independence in 1917. Based on the British Blue Ensign, it has four of the five stars of the Southern Cross.

Cook Islands
The flag has a circle of 15 stars – one for each island in the group – and was adopted in 1973 eight years after independence from New Zealand.

Niue
A self-governing dependency of New Zealand, Niue's bright yellow flag indicates warmth towards New Zealand and the Commonwealth.

Federated States of Micronesia
Formerly the Trust Territory of the Pacific Islands, these islands are administered by the United States. The four stars stand for the four territories.

Northern Marianas
A Commonwealth of the United States, its flag shows a white star in front of a *taga*, a chalice-shaped stone symbol of its ancient Polynesian inhabitants.

American Samoa
The islands are an American dependency and were granted their own government in 1960. The bald eagle holds a Samoan chief's staff and knife.

Guam
This island and base has been a dependency of the United States since 1898. The flag with its desert island picture is flown only with the US flag.

Papua New Guinea
The red and black flag is halved diagonally. A bird of paradise in flight is depicted in gold on the red and the stars of the Southern Cross constellation in white on the black.

Pitcairn
The flag of Britain's remaining dependency in the Pacific contains the coat of arms, which dates from 1969. The flag was adopted in 1984.

Flags of Europe

Switzerland
A square red flag with a white Greek Cross is the national flag of Switzerland, dating back to 1848. But the cross as the emblem of the Swiss is much older than this. In the 14th century, Swiss soldiers wore 'the sign of the Holy Cross, a white cross on a red shield'. The flag of the International Red Cross is based on the Swiss flag.

France
The colours of the French flag originated in the cockades worn during the revolution. They were adopted in 1789 and a flag incorporating them appeared in 1790. It was white, with a red, white and blue canton. In 1794 a call for a simpler flag, appropriate to republican morals, ideas and principles, resulted in the present tricolour.

Monaco
The colours of the flag come from the Prince of Monaco's coat of arms. Monaco has been an independent state since 980 AD but the present flag was adopted in 1881.

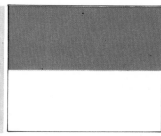

Belgium
The colours date from the arms of the Province of Brabant (a gold lion with red tongue on a black shield). Today's almost square flag was adopted in 1830 on independence from the Dutch.

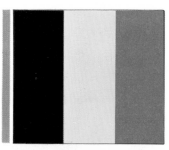

Netherlands
Before 1630, the followers of William of Orange flew an orange, white and blue flag. Red replaced the orange and the Dutch tricolour became a symbol of liberty.

Luxembourg
The flag of the Grand Duchy has similar colours to that of the Netherlands, but the flag is longer and the blue lighter. The colours were taken from the Grand Duke's 13th century coat of arms.

Ireland
First used by nationalists in the 1800's, green stands for the Catholics, orange for the Protestants and white for the much hoped for peace between them.

Liechtenstein

The colours date back to the early 19th century. The gold crown was added in 1937 to avoid confusion with the flag flown by Haiti at that time.

Federal Republic of Germany (West Germany)

The colours, dating back to the Holy Roman Empire and associated with the struggle for a united Germany from the 1830's, were re-adopted in 1949.

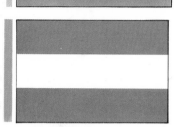

Austria

The flag was adopted in 1918 but the colours may date from the Battle of Ptolemais in 1191. It is said that the only part of the Duke of Bebenberg's white tunic not stained with blood was that under his sword belt.

United Kingdom

The Union flag combines English, Scottish and Irish emblems – but not one for Wales. The first Union flag dates from 1603, when James VI of Scotland became James I of England. The St. George's cross of England (1) and the St Andrew's cross of Scotland (3) formed the first Union flag. When Ireland was united with Great Britain in 1801, an Irish emblem was added to form the Union flag as we know it today. The red cross of St George has been used in England since the 13th century and St Andrew's flag of Scotland is probably even older. The white star in the centre of the flag of Northern Ireland (2) has six points representing the counties of Northern Ireland. The red dragon of Cadwallader, Prince of Gwynnedd, on a field of white and green, was officially recognised as the Welsh flag in 1959 (4).

1

2

3

4

Italy

When Napoleon invaded Italy in 1796, the French Guard had a standard of vertical green, white and red. The flag was finally established as that of a united Italy in 1861.

Vatican City

Situated inside Rome, this tiny state is the headquarters of the Roman Catholic Church. The flag bears the triple tiara of the Popes above the keys of heaven given to St Peter.

San Marino

The Republic has been an independent State since AD 885. The white is for the snowy mountains, the blue for the sky.

Portugal

The colours adopted in the revolution in 1910 represent Henry the Navigator (green) and the monarchy (red). The armillary shield – a navigational instrument – indicates Portugal's lead in exploration.

Spain

The flag of spain was adopted in 1785. Following a brief period during which the republican tricolour was in use, the present flag was re-adopted by General Franco in 1939.

Malta

The colours are from the arms of the Knights of St John. The George Cross was added in 1943, to commemorate the heroism of the Maltese in World War II. The present design dates from independence in 1964.

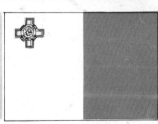

Gibraltar

Gibraltar, a UK dependency since 1713, flies the Union Flag officially, but the city flag symbolizing the fortified gateway to the Mediterranean is more often seen.

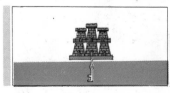

Greece

Since 1975 the national flag has been a white cross on a blue background. The striped flag – used from 1970 to 1975 – is now the civil and naval ensign.

Cyprus

Designed to avoid disunity between the Greek and Turkish communities on independence in 1960, the island is drawn over two olive branches. The separate communities fly the Greek and Turkish flags today.

Finland

The design was adopted when Finland gained independence from Russia in 1917. The Scandinavian blue cross is slightly off-centre towards the hoist.

Sweden

The flag of Sweden has been flown since the reign of King Gustavus in the 16th century, but was not officially adopted until 1906. The colours come from the state coat of arms dating back to 1364.

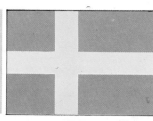

Norway

First adopted in 1821, the flag was not generally used until 1898. It is based on the flag of Denmark, to which Norway once belonged.

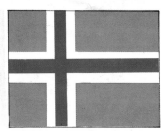

Denmark

Legend has it that King Waldemar II saw a white cross against a red sky in battle in 1219. His forces went on to win and the Dannebrog ('the spirit of Denmark') has been used continuously since.

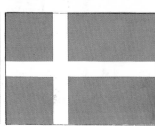

Faroe Islands

Adopted in 1948, the cross is like that on other Scandinavian flags – slightly off-centre. The Faroes remain part of the Danish realm.

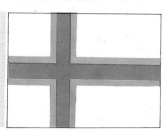

Iceland

Traditionally Iceland's colours are blue and white. The present colours are a combination of those of Denmark, Norway and the coat of arms. Dating from 1915, it became the official flag on independence in 1944.

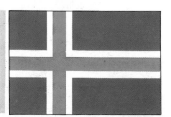

USSR (Soviet Union)

The plain red flag has the hammer (industry) and sickle (agriculture), together with the Communist Party star.

Poland

The red and white of Poland's flag come from the 13th century national emblem – a white eagle on a red field. The flag was adopted when Poland became a republic in 1919.

German Democratic Republic (East Germany)

In 1959 the state emblem of the German Democratic Republic was added to the old German flag (of 1949).

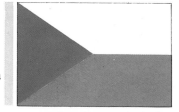

Czechoslovakia

The flag combines the red and white of Bohemia with blue – one of the colours of Moravia and Slovakia. First used in a horizontal tricolour by Slovakia in 1848, today's design dates from 1920.

Hungary

The Hungarian tricolour became popular in the revolution of 1848 and was adopted as that of independent Hungary in 1919 with the national arms in the centre. Since 1957 it has been without any central emblem.

COUNTRY	AREA Km2	POPULATION
EUROPE		
Albania	28,748	3,000,000
Austria	83,855	7,555,338
Belgium	30,518	9,857,721
Bulgaria	110,912	8,970,000
Cyprus	9,251	665,200
Czechoslovakia	127,903	15,500,000
Denmark	43,075	5,120,000
Faroe Islands	1,399	50,000
Finland	319,230	4,910,000
France	547,026	55,500,000
German Democratic Republic	108,333	16,600,000
Germany, Federal Republic of	248,706	61,020,000
Gibralter	6	28,843
Greece	131,957	9,970,000
Hungary	93,036	10,640,000
Iceland	102,819	242,089
Ireland, Republic of	70,283	3,540,000
Italy	301,268	87,200,000
Liechtenstein	160	27,076
Luxembourg	2,586	367,200
Malta	310	345,418
Monaco	1.9	27,063
Netherlands	40,844	14,530,000
Norway	386,877	4,200,000
Poland	312,683	37,000,000
Portugal	91,985	10,190,000
Romania	237,500	22,620,000
San Marino	61	22,418
Soviet Union (USSR)	22,402,200	281,700,000
Spain	504,750	39,300,000
Sweden	449,964	8,400,000
Switzerland	41,293	6,500,000
United Kingdom	229,880	56,490,00
Vatican City	0.44	1,000
Yugoslavia	255,804	23,120,000

Yugoslavia

In 1918 several states formed the new kingdom of Yugoslavia. The colours come from the flags of these states. In 1946 the coat of arms was replaced by the Communist star.

Romania

The colours come from the arms of the provinces that united to form Romania in 1861. The coat of arms shows the country's natural resources – forests, oil, wheat, mountains.

Bulgaria

A tricolour of white, green and red dates from 1878 – colours used in Slav countries at that time. The national emblem was first added to the flag in 1947. The lion has been a symbol of Bulgaria since the 14th century.

Albania

The name Albania means 'land of the eagle'. The flag bears a two-headed black eagle emblem on a dark red ground. The Communist star above the eagle was added in 1945.

Flags of Asia

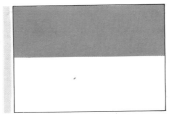

Indonesia

The red and white colours go back to the Middle Ages, a symbol of revolution then and of the struggle for independence in modern times. Indonesia became independent of the Netherlands in 1945.

Singapore

The flag dates from 1959 when self-government was introduced. The crescent stands for the young country's ascent and the stars for its aspirations to democracy, peace, progress, justice and equality.

Malaysia

The 14 stripes and points of the star stand for the 13 states and capital territory of Kuala Lumpur. The crescent and star are symbols of Islam.

Brunei

When the British took over in 1906 a white and a black stripe were added to the Sultan's plain yellow flag. In 1959 the state arms were added.

Philippines

The eight rays of the sun stand for the eight provinces that revolted against Spanish rule in 1898. The stars represent the three main island groups.

Thailand

Two red and white stripes are all that remain of Thailand's traditional red on white elephant emblem. The blue stripe, added in 1917, showed solidarity with the Allies, whose flags had the same colours.

Vietnam

A yellow star on a red field was the flag of Ho Chi-minh in World War II. In 1945 it became the national flag. Today, with a slight variation made to the star in 1955, it still flies over Vietnam – north and south.

Kampuchea (Cambodia)

The flag introduced by the current regime has been in general use since 1979. The red background symbolises revolution, while the silhouette is of the historic temple of Angkor Wat.

COUNTRY	AREA Km²	POPULATION
ASIA		
Afghanistan	652,090	17,150,000
Bahrain	676	435,065
Bangladesh	143,998	101,720,000
Bhutan	46,500	1,300,000
Brunei	5,765	221,900
Burma	678,000	37,610,000
China	9,572,900	1,049,710,000
Hong Kong	1,069	5,430,000
India	3,280,481	748,000,000
Indonesia	1,904,345	164,000,000
Iran	1,643,958	45,190,000
Iraq	434,923	15,400,000
Israel	20,770	4,230,000
Japan	372,313	121,050,000
Jordan	97,740	3,500,000
Kampuchea	181,035	6,230,000
Kuwait	17,819	1,770,000
Laos	236,800	3,723,000
Lebanon	10,400	3,500,000
Malaysia	329,752	16,100,000
Maldives	298	200,000
Mongolia	1,565,000	1,890,000
Nepal	140,797	16,630,000
North Korea	122,098	20,550,000
Oman	212,457	1,100,000
Pakistan	803,943	96,000,000
Philippines	300,000	56,210,000
Qatar	11,437	287,000
Saudi Arabia	2,149,690	11,520,000
Singapore	618	2,560,000
South Korea	99,022	41,800,000
Sri Lanka	65,610	15,840,000
Syria	185,180	10,960,000
Taiwan	36,179	19,135,000
Thailand	514,001	52,800,000
Turkey	779,452	50,670,000
United Arab Emirates	83,657	1,770,700
Vietnam	329,566	61,950,000
Yemen Arab Republic	195,000	7,880,000
Yemen People's Democratic Republic	287,682	2,500,000

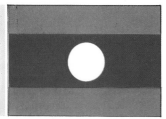

Laos

The flag of the Pathet Lao was adopted in 1975 when Laos became a Communist republic. The blue stands for the Mekong River, the white disc for the moon and the red for the unity and purpose of the people.

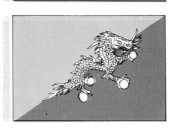

Burma

In 1974 a new socialist symbol appeared on the flag. A ring of 14 stars representing the 14 states surrounds a gearwheel and a rice plant, representing industry and agriculture.

Bhutan

The name Bhutan means 'Land of the Dragon', hence the strange creature in the middle of the flag. The saffron yellow colour represents royal power, and the orange-red represents Buddhist spiritual power.

Taiwan

Originally Sun Yat-sen's flag, the nationalists fought under the 'white sun in blue sky over red land' against the Communists. When they were forced to retreat to Taiwan, they took the flag with them.

China

Red – the traditional colour of China and of Communism – was chosen for the People's flag in 1949. The big star stands for the party's Common Programme, the small ones for the four social classes it unites.

Hong Kong

The British Blue Ensign has flown over Hong Kong since 1841. The coat of arms, dating from 1959, includes the British lion and Chinese dragon.

Mongolia

Communist red appears with blue, the Mongolian national colour. The gold star of the Communist Party tops the *soyonbo*, the traditional symbol of Mongolia.

North Korea

The Korean Democratic People's Republic was founded in 1948. The colours are those of the original flag, but in a new Communist pattern with a star.

South Korea

Adopted in 1950, the flag is the traditional white of peace. The central symbol stands for nature's opposing forces. The black symbols stand for the four seasons, the points of the compass and the sun, moon, earth and heaven.

Japan

The Land of the Rising Sun's flag was officially adopted in 1870 but it had been used by emperors in Japan for centuries before.

Nepal

This Himalayan kingdom has the only national flag that is not rectangular in shape. Two separate pennants were joined in the 19th century and the present design – retaining the crescent moon and sun – was adopted in 1962.

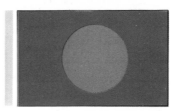

Afghanistan

After many recent changes, Afghanistan has reverted to its traditional colours with the state arms in the canton.

Bangladesh

Following the break with Pakistan in 1971, the new flag has a green field (for fertile land) and a red disc that represents the struggle for freedom.

Pakistan

Green is the traditional colour of Islam. The flag, adopted on independence in 1947, is green with the Muslim crescent and star. But a white stripe is left to represent the other religions and minorities.

India

Originally the Indian National Congress Flag, the orange represents the Hindu majority, green the Muslims, white the wish for peace between them. The Buddhist wheel symbol was added on independence in 1947.

Sri Lanka

The flag of this Buddhist nation includes the lion banner of the ancient kingdom, and two stripes for the island's minority groups, green for the Muslims, orange for the Hindus.

Maldives
The Republic of Maldives lies to the south-west of Sri Lanka. The flag has evolved over the years from a plain one to the present design, which was adopted in 1965.

Turkey
The crescent has appeared on flags of Turkey for centuries, but the star was added only in the mid 1800's. The flag was kept when the Ottoman Empire became the republic of Turkey in 1923.

Syria
Syria reverted to the flag of the former United Arab Republic in 1980, after severing its ties with Egypt. But both countries still use the same basic tricolour.

Lebanon
The cedar tree has been a symbol of Lebanon since the days of the Bible. The tree was included in the flag when the country became independent in 1943. The colours are those of the Lebanese Legion.

Israel
The blue and white stripes are from the Hebrew prayer-shawl and the Star of David is in the centre. Designed in the late 1800's, the flag was adopted by the new state in 1948.

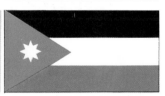

Jordan
Based on the flag of the Arab revolt, the present design was adopted in 1921. The points of the star stand for the first verses of the Koran.

Iraq
Designed in 1963 with the Pan-Arab colours, the idea was that Iraq, with Syria and Egypt, would have the same flag. The three stars stand for the three countries, but their unity is still awaited.

Iran
The flag of Iran contains the legend: 'Allah Akbar' repeated 22 times, to represent the date when the Ayatollah Khomeini took over. In the centre is the emblem of the Islamic revolution.

Saudi Arabia
The design was adopted in 1938. Above the white sword, the inscription reads: 'There is no god but Allah, and Muhammad is the Prophet of Allah'. The flag is double so that it can be read from both sides.

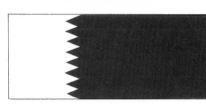

Bahrain
In 1820 the British requested friendly states around the Persian Gulf to have white on their flags. This is separated from the traditional Muslim red by a serrated line.

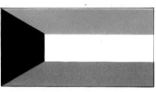

Qatar
The flag dates back to the mid-nineteenth century. Its maroon colour is said to represent the effect of the sun on its traditional red banner.

Kuwait
Independence was achieved in 1961, when Kuwait ceased to be a British Protectorate. The new flag has the four Pan-Arab colours.

United Arab Emirates
The Pan-Arab colours were a natural choice for the seven small states of the Persian Gulf which formed the United Arab Emirates in 1971.

Oman
Formerly Muscat and Oman, the state's flag was a traditional red. In 1970, when the State of Oman was established, the State arms of swords and a dagger were added with stripes of white and green.

Southern Yemen (People's Democratic Republic of Yemen)
The National Liberation Front's flag was red, white and black. When they forced the British to leave Aden in 1967, they added the pale blue triangle and red star.

Yemen (Yemen Arab Republic)
Like the people's republic, the flag is based on the Arab revolt flag (see Egypt). In 1962 the flag, with one green star, was adopted with Arab unity in mind.

INDEX

INDEX TO OUR WORLD

INDEX TO MAPS

Balearic Is. 28 H3
Balikpapan 42 E6
Balkan Mts. 33 J3
Balkhash, Lake 34 E5
Ballarat 55 G7
Ballater 24 F3
Ballina 25 B2
Ballinasloe 25 C3
Ballycastle 25 E1
Ballymena 25 E2
Ballyshannon 25 C2
Baltic Sea 29 G7
Baltimore 49 L4
Bamako 44 D3
Bamberg 30 D4
Banda Aceh 42 A4
Bandar Abbas 37 G4
Bandar-e-Lengeh 37 F4
Bandar Seri Begawan 42 D5
Bandirma 33 L4
Bandon 25 C5
Bandung 42 C7
Banff 24 F3
Bangalore 38 D6
Bangka 42 C6
Bankok 42 B3
Bangladesh 39 G4
Bangor (N. Ireland) 25 F2
Bangor (USA) 49 N3
Bangor (Wales) 22 C3
Bangui 45 F4
Banja Luka 32 F2
Banjarmasin 42 D6
Banjul 44 C3
Banks I. 46 D2
Bann 25 E2
Bantry 25 B5
Bantry Bay 25 B5
Baoding 41 J3
Baotou 41 G2
Bar 33 G3
Barbados 51 N5
Barbuda See Antigua-Barbuda
Barcaldine 55 H4
Barcelona 28 H2
Bareilly 38 D3
Barents Sea 34 D2
Bari 32 F4
Barisan Range 42 B6
Barkly Tableland 54 F3
Barlee Range 54 B4
Barnaul 34 F4
Barnsley 22 F3
Barnstable 23 C5
Barquisimeto 52 C1
Barra 24 A4
Barranquilla 52 B1
Barrow 25 E4
Barrow-in-Furness 22 D2
Barry 23 D5
Basel 27 H3
Basilan 43 F4
Basildon 23 H5
Basingstoke 23 F5
Basra 36 E3
Bassein 39 G5
Bass Strait 55 H7
Bastia 27 J5
Batangas 43 F3
Bath 23 E5
Bathurst Inlet 46 F3
Baton Rouge 49 H5
Battambang 42 B3
Battle Harbour 47 L6
Batumi 34 D5
Bauru 53 E5
Bayonne 26 D5
Bayreuth 30 D4

Beaufort Sea 46 C2
Beaufort West 44 M10
Beauvais 27 F2
Bedford 23 G4
Beijing (Peking) 41 J3
Beira 45 H6
Beirut 36 C3
Beitbridge 45 H7
Béja 28 C3
Belém 52 E3
Belfast 25 F2
Belfast Lough 25 F2
Belgaum 38 C5
Belgium 27
Belgrade 33 H2
Belitung 42 C6
Belize 50 G4
Belle Île 26 C3
Belo Horizonte 52 E4
Belukha, Mt. 34 F5
Bendigo 55 G7
Bengal, Bay of 39 F6
Bengbu 41 J4
Benghazi 45 G1
Benin 44 E3
Beni Suef 36 B4
Ben Macdhui 24 E3
Ben Nevis 24 D4
Benoni 44 N9
Benue 45 F4
Benxi 41 K2
Berbera 45 J3
Berezniki 34 D4
Bergama 33 L5
Bergamo 32 B2
Bergen 29 E6
Bergerac 26 E4
Berhampur 39 E5
Bering Sea 56 H1
Bering Strait 35 L3
Berlin 30 E2
Bermuda 51 M1
Berne 27 H3
Berwick-upon-Tweed 22 F1
Besançon 27 H3
Béziers 27 F5
Bhavnagar 38 C4
Bhopal 38 D4
Bhutan 39 G3
Bialystok 31 K2
Biarritz 26 D5
Bideford 23 C5
Bielefeld 30 C2
Bikaner 38 C3
Bilbao 28 E1
Billings 48 E2
Bioko I. 45 E4
Birdum 54 E3
Birjand 37 G3
Birkenhead 22 D3
Birmingham (England) 22 F4
Birmingham (USA) 49 J5
Biscay, Bay of 26
Biskra 45 E1
Bismarck 48 F2
Bismarck Sea 43 K6
Bissau 44 C3
Bitola 33 H4
Bizerte 45 E1
Blackburn 22 E3
Black Forest 30 C4
Blackpool 22 D3
Black Sea 21 G4
Blackwater 25 C4
Blagoevgrad 33 J3
Blagoveshchensk 35 H4
Blanc, Mont 32 A2
Blantyre 45 H6

Blenheim 55 N10
Blida 44 E1
Bloemfontein 44 N9
Blue Nile 45 H3
Blyth 22 F1
Boa Vista 52 C2
Bobo-Dioulasso 44 D3
Bochum 30 B3
Bodmin Moor 23 C6
Bodö 29 F5
Bognor Regis 23 G6
Bogor 42 C7
Bogotá 52 B2
Bohemian Forest 30 E4
Boise 48 C3
Bolivia 52 C4
Bologna 32 C2
Bolsena, Lake 32 C3
Bolshevik 35 G2
Boshoi Lyakhovskiy 35 J2
Bolton 22 E3
Bombay 38 C5
Bonifacio 32 B4
Bonn 30 B3
Borås 29 F7
Bordeaux 26 D4
Borneo 42 D6
Bornholm 29 F7
Bosa 32 B4
Boston (England) 22 G4
Boston (USA) 49 M3
Botasani 33 L1
Bothia, Gulf of 47 G2
Bothnia, Gulf of 29 H6
Botswana 45 G7
Bouaké 44 D4
Boulogne 27 E1
Bourges 27 F3
Bourke 55 H5
Bournemouth 23 F6
Bowen 55 H3
Bradford 22 F3
Braemar 24 E4
Braga 28 B2
Brahmaputra 39 G3
Braila 33 L2
Brandon 46 F7
Brantford 47 H8
Brasilia 52 E4
Brasov 33 K2
Bratislava 31 G4
Bratsk 35 G4
Brazil 52 D3
Brazilian Highlands 52 E4
Brazzaville 45 F5
Brechin 24 F4
Brecon 23 D5
Brecon Beacons 23 D5
Breidha Fjördhur 29 A2
Bremen 30 C2
Bremerhaven 30 C2
Brescia 32 C2
Brest (France) 26 B2
Brest (USSR) 34 C4
Bridgwater 23 D5
Bridlington 22 G2
Brighton 23 G6
Brisbane 55 J5
Bristol 23 E5
Bristol Channel 23 C5
British Columbia 46 D6
British Virgin Is. 51 M4
Brno 31 G4
Broadford 24 C3
Broads, The 22 J4
Brod 32 G2
Broken Hill 55 G6
Broome 54 C3

Brownsville 48 G6
Brunei 42 D5
Brunswick 30 D2
Brussels 27 G1
Bryansk 34 C4
Bucaramanga 52 B2
Bucharest 33 L2
Budapest 31 H5
Buenos Aires 53 D6
Buffalo 49 L3
Bujumbura 45 G5
Bukavu 45 G5
Bukhara 34 E6
Bulawayo 45 G7
Bulgaria 33
Bulun 35 H2
Bunbury 54 B6
Buncrana 25 D1
Bundaberg 55 J4
Burdwan 39 F4
Burgas 33 L3
Burgos 28 E1
Burkina Faso 44 D3
Burlington 49 M3
Burma 39 H4
Burnley 22 E3
Bursa 33 M4
Burton upon Trent 22 F4
Buru 43 G6
Burundi 45 G5
Bury St. Edmunds 23 H4
Bushire 37 F4
Butuan 43 G4
Buxton 22 F3
Bydgoszcz 31 G2
Byrd Land 59 P3

C
Cabanatuan 43 F2
Cabimas 52 B1
Cabinda 45 F5
Cadiz (Philippines) 43 F3
Cádiz (Spain) 28 C4
Cádiz, Gulf of 28 C4
Caen 26 D2
Caernarfon 22 C3
Cagayan de Oro 43 F4
Cagliari 32 B5
Cairngorms 24 E3
Cairns 55 H3
Cairo 36 B3
Calabar 45 E4
Calais 27 E1
Calbayog 43 F3
Calcutta 39 F4
Calgary 46 E6
Cali 52 B2
Calicut 38 D6
California 48 C4
California, Gulf of 50 B2
Callander 24 D4
Callao 52 B4
Calvi 27 J5
Camagüey 51 J3
Cambay, Gulf of 38 C4
Cambodia See Kampuchea
Cambrian Mts. 23 D4
Cambridge 23 H4
Cameroon 45 F4
Campbeltown 24 C5
Campeche Bay 50 F4
Campina Grande 52 F3
Campinas 53 E5
Campo Grande 52 D5
Cam Ranh 42 C3
Canada 46
Canakkale 33 L4
Canary Is. 44 C2

Canberra 55 H7
Canea 33 K7
Cannes 27 H5
Cantabrian Mts. 28 D1
Canterbury 23 J5
Can Tho 42 C3
Canton *See* Guangzhou
Cape Town 44 L10
Cape Verde Is. 44 B3
Capri 32 E4
Capricorn, Tropic of 54 C4
Caracal 33 K2
Caracas 52 C1
Carcassonne 27 F5
Cardiff 23 D5
Cardigan 23 C4
Cardigan Bay 23 C4
Caribbean Sea 51 K5
Carlisle 22 E2
Carlow 25 E4
Carmarthen 23 C5
Carnarvon 54 A4
Caroline Is. 56 D6
Carpathian Mts. 33 K1
Carpentaria, Gulf of 55 F2
Carrantuohill 25 B4
Carrickmacross 25 E3
Carrick-on-Shannon 25 C3
Carson City 48 C4
Cartagena (Colombia) 52 B1
Cartagena (Spain) 28 F4
Caruaru 52 F3
Casablanca 44 D1
Cascade Range 48 B3
Cashel 25 D4
Caspian Sea 34 D5
Castellón de la Plana 28 F3
Castlebar 25 B3
Catania 32 E6
Caucasus Mts. 34 D5
Caxias do Sul 53 D5
Cayenne 52 D2
Cayman Is. 51 H4
Cebu 43 F3
Cedar Rapids 49 H3
Ceduna 54 E6
Celebes Sea 43 F5
Central African Republic 45 G4
Central Russian Uplands 21 G3
Central Siberian Plateau 35 G3
Ceram 43 G6
Ceuta (Morocco) 44 D1
Ceuta (Spain) 28 D5
Cévennes 27 F4
Chad 45 F3
Chad, Lake 45 F3
Chah Bahar 37 H4
Challanger Deep 56 D5
Châlons-sur-Marne 27 G2
Chalon-sur-Saône 27 G3
Chandigarh 38 D2
Changchun 41 L2
Chang Jiang (Yangtze) 41 H4
Changsha 41 H5
Channel Is. 26 C2
Chardzhou 34 E6
Charikar 37 J3
Charleroi 27 G1
Charleston (W. Va.) 49 K4
Charleston (S. Carolina) 49 L5
Charleville 55 H5
Charleville-Mézières 30 A4
Charlotte 49 K4
Charlottetown 47 K7
Chartres 26 E2
Châteauroux 27 E3
Châtellerault 26 E3
Chatham Is. 56 H11

Chattanooga 49 J4
Cheboksary 34 D4
Chelmsford 23 H5
Cheltenham 23 E5
Chelyabinsk 34 E4
Chengdu 40 F4
Cherbourg 26 D2
Cheremkhovo 35 G4
Cherepovets 34 C4
Chernyakhovsk 31 J1
Cherskogo Range 35 J3
Chester 22 E3
Chesterfield 23 F3
Chesterfield Inlet 47 G4
Cheviot Hills 23 E1
Cheyenne 48 F3
Chiang Mai 42 A2
Chiba 43 O3
Chicago 49 J3
Chichester 23 G6
Chiclayo 52 B3
Chicoutimi 47 J7
Chihuahua 50 C2
Chile 53 B5
Chillán 53 B6
Chiltern Hills 23 G5
Chimborazo 52 B3
Chimbote 52 B3
Chimkent 34 E5
China 40
Chingola 45 G6
Chita 35 G4
Chittagong 39 G4
Chojnice 31 G2
Cholet 26 D3
Chongjin 41 L2
Chonju 41 L3
Chorzów 31 H3
Christchurch 55 N10
Chukchi Sea 58 B2
Chungking 40 G5
Chur 27 J3
Churchill 46 G5
Ciénaga 52 B1
Cienfuegos 51 H3
Cincinnati 49 K4
Cinto, Mt. 32 B3
Ciudad Bolivar 52 C2
Ciudad Guayana 52 C2
Ciudad Juárez 50 C1
Ciudad Obregón 50 C2
Clara 25 D3
Cleethorpes 22 G3
Clermont Ferrand 27 F4
Cleveland 49 K3
Clifden 25 A3
Clipperton I. 57 Q5
Clonmet 25 D4
Ciuj 33 J1
Clyde 24 E5
Clydebank 24 D5
Coastal Mts. 46 D6
Coastal Range 48 B3
Coatbridge 24 D5
Coats Land 59 A3
Cobh 25 C5
Cochabamba 52 C4
Cochin 38 D6
Cognac 26 D4
Coimbatore 38 D6
Coimbra 28 B2
Colchester 23 H5
Coleraine 25 E1
Coll 24 B4
Cologne 30 B3
Colombia 52 B2
Colombo 38 D7

Colón 51 J6
Colorado 48 E4
Colorado R. 48 D4
Colorado Plateau 48 E4
Colorado Springs 48 F4
Columbia 49 K5
Columbus (Georgia) 49 K5
Columbus (Ohio) 49 K4
Colwyn Bay 22 D3
Communism Peak 34 E6
Como, Lake 32 B2
Comodoro Rivadavia 53 C7
Comoro Is. 45 J6
Conakry 44 C4
Concepción (Chile) 53 B6
Concepción (Paraguay) 53 D5
Concordia 53 D6
Congo 45 F5
Conn, Lough 25 B2
Connah's Quay 22 D3
Connecticut 49 M3
Constance, Lake 30 C5
Constanta 33 M2
Constantine 45 E1
Cook, Mt. 55 N10
Cook Is. 56 J9
Cook Strait 55 N10
Cooktown 55 H3
Coolgardie 54 C6
Copenhagen 29 F7
Coppermine 46 E3
Coral Sea 56 D8
Córdoba (Argentina) 53 C6
Córdoba (Spain) 28 D4
Corfu 33 G5
Corinth 33 J6
Cork 25 C5
Corner Brook 47 L7
Corpus Christi 48 G6
Corrib, Lough 25 B3
Corrientes 53 D5
Corsica 27 J5
Corte 32 B3
Cosenza 32 F5
Costa Rica 51 H5
Cotswold 23 E5
Cottbus 31 F3
Coventry 23 F4
Covilhã 28 C2
Craiova 33 J2
Crete 33 K7
Crete, Sea of 33 K6
Crewe 22 E3
Cromarty 24 D3
Cromer 22 J4
Croydon 23 G5
Cuba 51 J3
Cúcuta 52 B2
Cuddalore 38 D6
Cuenca 52 B3
Cuenca, Serrania de 28 F2
Cuiabá 52 D4
Culiacan 50 C3
Cumaná 52 C1
Cumbernauld 24 E5
Curitiba 53 E5
Cuttack 39 F4
Cuzco 52 B4
Cyprus 36 B2
Czechoslovakia 31
Czestochowa 31 H3

D
Dakar 44 C3
Dallas 49 G5
Damascus 36 C3
Dampier 54 B4

Da Nang 42 C2
Danube 33 L2
Dar-es-Salaam 45 H5
Darjeeling 39 F3
Darling 55 G6
Darlington 22 F2
Darmstadt 30 C4
Dartmoor 23 C6
Daru 43 K7
Darwin 54 E2
Dasht-e-Kavir 37 F3
Dasht-e-Lut 37 G3
Datong 41 H2
Daugavpils 29 J7
Davao 43 G4
Davenport 49 H3
Davis Strait 47 L3
Davos 32 B1
Dawson 46 C4
Dax 26 D5
Dayton 49 K4
Dead Sea 36 C3
Death Valley 48 C4
Debrecan 31 J5
Decatur 49 J4
Deccan 38 D5
Dee 22 D4
Dehra Dun 38 D2
Dej 33 J1
Delaware 49 L4
Delhi 38 D3
Demavend 37 F2
Denbigh 22 D3
Denmark 29 E7
Denver 48 F4
Derby (Australia) 54 C3
Derby (England) 22 F4
Derg, Lough 25 C4
Des Moines 49 H3
Dessau 30 E3
Detroit 49 K3
Devon I. 47 H1
Devonport 55 H8
Dhaka 39 G4
Dhanbad 39 F4
Dieppe 26 E2
Dijon 27 G3
Dinaric Alps 32 F2
Dingle 25 A4
Dingle Bay 25 A4
Dingwall 24 D3
Diredawa 45 J4
Diyarbakir 36 D2
Djibouti 45 J3
Dnepropetrovsk 34 C5
Dnestr 21 F3
Dnieper 34 C4
Dodoma 45 H5
Doha 37 F4
Dolomites 32 C1
Dombàs 29 E6
Dominica 51 M4
Dominican Republic 51 L4
Don (Scotland) 24 F3
Don (USSR) 34 D5
Doncaster 22 F3
Donegal 25 C2
Donegal Bay 25 C2
Donetsk 34 C5
Dongola 36 B6
Dorchester 23 E6
Dordogne 26 E4
Dore. Mt. 27 F4
Dortmund 30 B3
Douai 27 F1
Douala 45 E4

Kalinin 34 C4
Kaliningrad 34 C4
Kalisz 31 H3
Kalmar 29 G7
Kamchatka Penisula 35 J4
Kampala 45 H4
Kampot 42 B3
Kampuchea 42 C3
Kananga 45 G5
Kanazawa 41 N3
Kanchenjunga 39 F3
Kandahar 37 J3
Kandalaksha 29 K5
Kangaroo I. 54 F7
Kankan 44 D3
Kano 45 E3
Kanpur 38 E3
Kansas 48 G4
Kansas City 49 H4
Kansk 35 F4
Kapfenberg 32 E1
Karachi 38 B4
Karaganda 34 E5
Karakoram Pass 38 D1
Karakoram Range 38 D1
Kara Sea 34 E2
Karbala 36 D3
Karl Marx Stadt 30 E3
Karlovac 32 E2
Karlovy Vary 30 E3
Karlskrona 29 G7
Karlsruhe 30 C4
Karlstad 29 F7
Karnobat 33 L3
Karpáthos 33 L7
Kasai 45 F5
Kasama 45 H6
Kassala 36 C6
Kassel 30 C3
Kastoria 33 H4
Katherine 54 E2
Kathmandu 39 E3
Katoomba 55 J6
Katowice 31 H3
Katsina 45 E3
Kauai 56 K4
Kaunas 31 K1
Kawasaki 41 N3
Kayseri 36 C2
Kazan 34 D4
Kéa 33 K6
Kebnekaise 29 G5
Kecskemet 31 H5
Kediri 42 D7
Kefallinía 33 H5
Keflavik 29 A3
Keighley 22 F3
Keith 24 F3
Kékes 31 J5
Kells 25 E3
Kemerovo 34 F4
Kemi 29 H5
Kemi R. 29 J5
Kemp Land 59 E3
Kempten 30 D5
Kendal 22 E2
Kendari 43 F6
Kenmare 25 B5
Kenora 46 G7
Kentucky 49 J4
Kenya 45 H4
Kenya. Mt. 45 H4
Kerintji 42 B6
Kerman 37 G3
Kesan 33 L4

Keswick 22 D2
Kettering 23 G4
Khabarovsk 35 H5
Khaburah 37 G5
Khairpur 38 B3
Khalkis 33 J5
Kharkov 34 C4
Khartoum 36 B6
Khartoum North 36 B6
Kherson 34 C5
Khíos 33 L5
Khorramabad 36 E3
Khorramshahr 36 E3
Khulna 39 F4
Khyber Pass 37 K3
Kiev 34 C4
Kigali 45 H5
Kikinda 33 H2
Kitwit 45 F5
Kildare 25 E3
Kilimanjaro. Mt. 45 H5
Kilkee 25 B4
Kilkenny 25 D4
Kilkis 33 J4
Killarney 25 B4
Kilmarnock 24 D5
Kilrush 25 B4
Kimberley 44 M9
Kimberley Plateau 54 D3
King Edward VII Land 59 N3
King I. 55 G7
King's Lynn 22 H4
Kingston 51 J4
Kingston upon Hull 22 G3
Kinshasa 45 F5
Kirgiz Steppe 21 J3
Kiribati 56 G7
Kirkcaldy 24 E4
Kirkenes 29 K5
Kirklareli 33 L4
Kirkuk 36 D2
Kirkwall 24 F2
Kirov 34 D4
Kirovabad 36 E1
Kiruna 29 H5
Kisangani 45 G4
Kishinev 34 C5
Kisumu 45 H5
Kitakyushu 41 M4
Kitchener 47 H8
Kíthira 33 J6
Kithnos 33 K6
Kitwe 45 G6
Kizil 36 C2
Klagenfurt 31 F5
Klaipeda 29 H7
Knoxville 49 K4
Kobe 41 N4
Koblenz 30 B3
Kola 29 K5
Kolding 29 E7
Kolguyev 34 D3
Kolhapur 38 C5
Kolobrzeg 31 F1
Kolwezi 45 G6
Kolyma Range 35 K3
Komotini 33 K4
Komsomolets 35 F1
Komsomolsk-na-Amur 35 H4
Konya 36 B2
Kopet Range 37 G2
Korce 33 H4
Kos 33 L6
Kosciusko. Mt. 55 H7
Kosice 31 J4

Kostroma 34 D4
Kostrzyn 31 F2
Koszalin 31 G1
Kota 38 D3
Kota Baharu 42 B4
Kota Kinabalu 44 E4
Kotelnyy 35 H2
Kotka 29 J6
Kotor 33 G3
Kowloon 41 H6
Kragujevac 33 H2
Krakow 31 H3
Krasnodar 34 C5
Krasnoyarsk 35 F4
Kratie 42 C3
Krems 31 F4
Kristiansand 29 E7
Krivoy Rog 34 C5
Kroonstad 44 N9
Krugersdorp 44 N9
Kuala Lumpur 42 B5
Kuching 42 D5
Kudat 42 E4
Kufstein 32 D1
Kumamoto 41 M4
Kumasi 44 D5
Kunlun Shan 39 F1
Kunming 40 F5
Kuopio 29 J6
Kupang 43 F8
Kurgan 34 E4
Kuril Is. 35 J5
Kurnool 38 D5
Kursk 34 C4
Kustanay 34 E4
Kuwait 36 E4
Kuybyshev 34 D4
Kwangju 41 L3
Kweiyang 40 G5
Kyle of Lochalsh 24 C3
Kyluchevskaya 35 K4
Kyoto 41 N3
Kyushu 41 M4

L
Labrador 47 K6
La Coruña 28 B1
Ladysmith 44 M10
Lagos (Nigeria) 44 E4
Lagos (Portugal) 28 B4
Lahore 38 C2
Lahti 29 J6
Lairg 24 D2
Lake District 22 D2
Lakselv 29 H4
Lakshadweep Is. 38 C6
Lamía 33 J5
Lancaster 22 E2
Lancaster Sound 47 H2
Lanchow 40 F3
Landeck 32 C1
Land's End 23 B6
Lansing 49 K3
Laoag 42 F2
Lao Cai 42 B1
Laos 42 C2
La Paz 52 C4
Lapland 29 H5
La Plata 53 D6
La Plata, Rio de 53 D6
Laptev Sea 35 H2
Lárisa 33 J5
Larne 25 F2
La Roshe-sur-Yon 26 D3
Las Palmas 44 C2
La Spezia 32 B2
Las Vegas 48 C4

Latakia 36 C2
Lauchhammer 30 E3
Launceston 55 H8
Lausanne 27 H3
Leamington Spa 23 F4
Lebanon 36 C3
Leeds 22 F3
Legnica 31 G3
Leh 38 D2
Le Havre 26 E2
Leicester 22 F4
Leipzig 30 E3
Le Mans 26 E3
Lena 35 H3
Leninabad 34 E5
Leningrad 34 C4
Lens 27 F1
Leoben 31 F5
León 50 D3
Léon 28 D1
Le Puy 27 F4
Lérida 28 G2
Lerwick 24 A1
Les Ecrins 27 H4
Leskovac 33 H3
Lesotho 44 N9
Lesser Antilles 51 M5
Lesser Sundra Is. 42 E7
Lésvos 33 L5
Leszno 31 G3
Lethbridge 46 E7
Lewis 24 B2
Lexington 49 K4
Leyte 43 G3
Lhasa 39 G3
Liaoyuan 41 L2
Liberec 31 F3
Liberia 44 D4
Libreville 45 E4
Libya 45 F2
Libyan Desert 45 F3
Liechtenstein 30 C5
Liège 27 G1
Lienz 32 D1
Liepaja 29 H7
Liffey 25 E3
Ligurian Sea 32 B3
Likasi 45 G6
Lille 27 F1
Lillehammer 29 F6
Lilongwe 45 H6
Lima 52 B4
Limerick 25 C4
Límnos 33 K5
Limoges 26 E4
Limpopo 44 N8
Linares 28 E3
Lincoln 22 G3
Lindos 33 M6
Line Is. 56 J6
Linköping 29 G7
Linz 31 F4
Lions, Gulf of 27 G5
Lipari Is. 32 E5
Lisbon 28 B3
Lisburn 25 E2
Lismore 55 J5
Little Rock 49 H5
Liuzhou 41 G6
Liverpool 22 E3
Livingstone 45 G6
Livorno 32 C3
Lizard Point 23 B7
Ljubljana 32 E1
Llandrindod Wells 23 D4
Llandudno 22 D3
Llanelli 23 C5

Lobito 45 F6
Locarno 32 B2
Łódź 31 H3
Lofoten Is. 29 F5
Logan. Mt. 46 B4
Logroño 28 E1
Loire 26 D3
Lom 33 J3
Lombok 42 E7
Lomé 44 E4
Lomond, Loch 24 D4
Lomza 31 K2
London (Canada) 49 H8
London (England) 23 G5
Londonderry 25 D2
Londrina 53 D5
Long Beach 48 C5
Longford 25 D3
Lorient 26 C3
Los Angeles 48 C5
Lot 26 E4
Loughborough 22 F4
Louisiana 49 H5
Louis Trichardt 44 N8
Louisville 49 J4
Lourdes 26 D5
Lower Lough Erne 25 D2
Lowestoft 22 J4
Luanda 45 F5
Luang Prabang 42 B2
Luanshya 45 G6
Lubango 45 F6
Lübeck 30 D2
Lublin 31 K3
Lubumbashi 45 G6
Lucknow 38 E3
Lüda 41 K3
Ludhiana 38 D2
Lugo 28 C1
Lugoj 33 H2
Lule 29 H5
Luleå 29 H5
Luleburgaz 33 L4
Luoyang 41 H4
Lurgan 25 E2
Lusaka 45 G6
Luton 23 G5
Luxembourg 30 B4
Luxor 36 B4
Luzern 27 J3
Luzon 43 F2
Luzon Strait 43 F2
Lvov 34 C5
Lyon 27 G4

M
Maas 30 A3
Maastricht 30 A3
Macapá 52 D2
Macau 41 H6
McClintock Channel 46 F2
McClure Strait 46 E2
Macdonnell Range 54 E4
Maceió 52 F3
Machilipatnam 38 E5
Mackay 55 H4
Mackenzie 46 D4
Mackenzie Mts. 46 C4
McKinley, Mt. 46 A4
Macomer 32 B4
Mâcon 27 G3
Mac Robertson Land 59 F2
Madagascar, Democratic
  Republic of 45 J7
Madeira 44 C1
Madeira R. 52 C3
Madison 49 J3
Madras 38 E6

Madrid 28 E2
Madurai 38 D7
Mafikeng 44 N9
Magadan 35 J4
Magdeburg 30 D2
Magellan, Strait of 53 C8
Maggiore, Lake 32 B2
Magnitogorsk 34 D4
Mahajanga 45 J6
Maidstone 23 H5
Maidurguri 45 F3
Main 30 D3
Maine 49 N2
Mainz 30 C4
Majene 42 E6
Majorca 28 H3
Makassar Strait 42 E6
Makhachkala 34 D5
Malabo 45 E4
Malacca, Strait of 42 B5
Málaga 28 D4
Malagasy, Republic of
  See Madagascar
Malang 42 D7
Malange 45 F5
Mälaren, Lake 29 G7
Malatya 36 C2
Malawi 45 H6
Malawi, Lake 45 H6
Malaysia 42
Malbork 31 H1
Malegaon 38 C4
Mali 44 D3
Mallow 25 C4
Malmö 29 F7
Malta 32 E7
Manado 43 F5
Managua 51 G5
Manama 37 F4
Manaus 52 D3
Manchester 22 E3
Mandala Peak 43 K6
Mandalay 39 H4
Mandurah 54 B6
Mangalia 33 M3
Mangalore 38 C6
Manila 42 F3
Manisa 33 L5
Manitoba 46 G5
Manizales 52 B2
Mansfield 22 F3
Maoke Range 43 J6
Maputo 44 P9
Maracaibo 52 B1
Maracay 52 C1
Maragheh 36 E2
Marañón 52 B3
Maras 36 C2
Marathon 33 J5
Marbella 28 D4
Mar Del Plata 53 D6
Mardin 36 D2
Margate 23 J5
Marianao 51 H3
Marianas 56 D5
Maribor 32 E1
Maritsa 33 K3
Marmara, Sea of 33 M4
Marmaris 33 M6
Marne 27 F2
Marquesas Is. 57 M7
Marrakesh 44 D1
Marseille 27 G5
Marshall Is. 56 G6
Martaban, Gulf of 39 H5
Martinique 51 M5
Maryborough 55 J5
Maryland 49 L4

Masan 41 L3
Maseru 44 N9
Mashhad 37 G2
Mask, Lough 25 B3
Massachusetts 49 M3
Massawa 45 H3
Massif Central 27 F4
Masterton 55 O10
Masvingo 45 H7
Matadi 45 F5
Matamoros 50 E2
Mathura 38 D3
Mato Grosso 52 D4
Matruh 36 A3
Matsuyama 41 M4
Matterhorn 32 A2
Maui 56 K4
Mauritania 44 C3
Mazar-i-Sharif 37 J2
Mazatlán 50 C3
Mbabane 44 P9
Mbandaka 45 F4
Mbuju Mayi 45 G5
Mecca 36 C5
Medan 42 A5
Medellín 52 B2
Medina 36 C5
Meerut 38 D3
Meissen 30 E3
Meknès 44 D1
Mekong 42 B2
Melbourne 55 G7
Melville I. (Australia) 54 E2
Melville I. (Canada) 46 E1
Memmingen 30 D5
Memphis 49 J4
Mendi 43 K7
Mendoza 53 C6
Merauke 43 K7
Mergui Archipelago 39 H6
Mérida (Mexico) 50 G3
Mérida (Spain) 28 C3
Mersin 36 B2
Merthyr Tydfil 23 D5
Meseta 20 C4
Mesolóngion 33 H5
Messina 32 E5
Metković 32 F3
Metz 27 H2
Meuse 27 G1
Mexicali 50 A1
Mexico 50
Mexico, Gulf of 50 F2
Mexico City 50 E4
Mezenc, Mt. 27 G4
Miami 51 H2
Michigan 49 J2
Michigan, Lake 49 J3
Micronesia 56
Middlesbrough 22 F2
Midway Is. 56 H4
Midye 33 M4
Milan 32 B2
Milâs 33 L6
Milford Haven 23 B5
Milos 33 K6
Milton Keynes 23 G5
Milwaukee 49 J3
Mindanao 43 G4
Mindoro 42 F3
Minneapolis 49 H2
Minnesota 49 H2
Minorca 28 J3
Minsk 34 C4
Miquelon 47 L7
Mirzapur 39 E3
Miskolc 31 J4
Misool 43 H6

Mississippi 49 J5
Mississippi R. 49 H3
Missouri 49 H4
Missouri R. 48 E2
Misurata 45 F1
Mitchell, Mt. 49 K4
Mitilíni 33 L5
Miyazaki 41 M4
Mobile 49 J5
Moçambique 45 J6
Modena 32 C2
Moffat 24 E5
Mogadishu 45 J4
Moluccas 43 G6
Mombasa 45 H5
Monaco 32 A3
Monaghan 25 E2
Mönchen-Gladbach 30 B3
Moncton 47 K7
Monghyr 39 F3
Mongolia 35 G5
Mongu 45 G6
Monroe 49 H5
Monrovia 44 C4
Mons 27 F1
Montana 43 E2
Montargis 27 F3
Montauban 26 E5
Montélimar 27 G4
Monteria 52 B2
Monterrey 50 D2
Montevideo 53 D6
Montgomery 49 J5
Montluçon 27 F3
Montpellier 27 F5
Montreal 47 J7
Montreux 27 H3
Montrose 24 F4
Monza 32 B2
Moora 54 B6
Moorea 57 L8
Moose Jaw 46 F6
Mora 29 F6
Moradabad 38 D3
Moray Firth 24 E3
Morecambe 22 E2
Morelia 50 D4
Morlaix 26 C2
Morocco 44 D1
Morwell 55 H7
Moscow 34 C4
Mosel 30 B4
Mossel Bay 44 M10
Mostar 32 F3
Mosul 36 D2
Motala 29 F7
Motherwell 24 E5
Moulmein 39 H5
Mount Gambier 55 G7
Mount Isa 55 F4
Mount Magnet 54 B5
Mount Newman 54 B4
Mozambique 45 H6
Mozambique Channel 45 J6
Mukachevo 31 K4
Mukalla 36 E7
Mulhacén 28 E4
Mulhouse 27 H3
Mull 24 C4
Multan 38 C2
Munich 30 D4
Münster 30 B3
Murcia 28 F4
Mures 33 J1
Murmansk 34 C3
Murray 55 G7
Murud 42 E5
Muscat 37 G5

Pec 33 H3
Pechenga 29 K5
Pechora 21 J1
Pécs 31 H5
Peebles 24 E5
Pegu 39 H5
Peking *See* Beijing
Pelotas 53 D6
Pematangsiantar 42 A5
Pemba 45 J6
Pemba I. 45 H5
Pembroke 23 C5
Pennines 22 E2
Pennsylvania 49 L3
Penrith 22 E2
Pentland Firth 24 E2
Penza 34 D4
Penzance 23 B6
Peoria 49 J3
Pereira 52 B2
Périgueux 26 E4
Perm 34 D4
Perpignan 27 F5
Perth (Australia) 54 B6
Perth (Scotland) 24 E4
Peru 52 B4
Pescara 32 E3
Peshawar 38 C2
Peterborough (Canada) 47 J8
Peterborough (England) 22 G4
Peterhead 24 G3
Petrich 33 J4
Petropavlovsk 34 E4
Petropavlovsk 35 J4
Patrópolis 53 E5
Petrozavodsk 34 C3
Philadelphia 49 L3
Philippines 43
Phnom Penh 42 B3
Phoenix 48 D5
Phoenix Is. 56 H7
Phuket 42 A4
Pierre 48 F3
Pietermaritzburg 44 P9
Pietersburg 44 N8
Pila 31 G2
Pilos 33 H6
Pindus Mts. 33 H5
Pines. I. of 51 H3
Piraeus 33 J6
Pírgos 33 H6
Pisa 32 C3
Pitcairn I. 57 M9
Pitesti 33 K2
Pitlochry 24 E4
Pittsburg 49 L3
Piura 52 A3
Pleven 33 K3
Ploesti 33 L2
Plovdiv 33 K3
Plymouth 23 C6
Plzen 30 E4
Po 32 C2
Pointe Noire 45 F5
Poitiers 26 E3
Poland 31
Polynesia 56
Ponce 51 L4
Pontianak 42 C6
Pontine Mts. 36 C1
Pontypool 23 D5
Pontypridd 23 D5
Poole 23 F6
Poopó, Lake 52 C4
Popocatépetl 50 E4
Portadown 25 E2
Port Arthur 49 H5

Port Augusta 54 F6
Port-au-Prince 51 K4
Port Bou 28 H1
Port Elizabeth 44 N10
Port-Gentil 45 F5
Port Harcourt 44 E4
Port Hedland 54 B4
Portland 48 B2
Port Laoise 25 D3
Port Lincoln 54 F6
Port Macquarie 55 J6
Pórto Alegre 53 D5
Port of Spain 52 C1
Porto-Novo 44 E4
Port Pirie 54 F6
Portree 24 B3
Portrush 25 E1
Port Said 36 B3
Portsmouth 23 F6
Port Sudan 36 C6
Port Talbot 23 D5
Portugal 28
Po-Shan 41 J3
Potchefstroom 44 N9
Potosí 52 C4
Potsdam 30 E2
Poznań 31 G2
Prague 31 F3
Prespa, Lake 33 H4
Peston 22 E3
Prestwick 24 D5
Pretoria 44 N9
Préveza 33 H5
Prince Charles I. 47 J3
Prince Edward I. 47 K7
Prince George 46 D6
Prince of Wales I. 46 G2
Princess Elizabeth Land 59 G3
Principe 45 E4
Pristina 33 H3
Prokopyevsk 34 F4
Providence 49 M3
Provo 48 D3
Przemyśl 31 K4
Pskov 34 C4
Puebla 50 E4
Pueblo 48 F4
Puerto Montt 53 B7
Puerto Rico 51 L4
Pultusk 31 J2
Puncak Jaya 43 J6
Pune 38 C5
Punta Arenas 53 B8
Pusan 41 L3
Pwllheli 22 C4
Pyongyang 41 L3
Pyrénées 28 G1

Q
Qahremanshahr 36 E3
Qatar 37 F4
Qattara Depression 45 G2
Qazvin 36 E2
Quingdao 41 K3
Quiqihar 41 K1
Qishn 37 F6
Qom 37 F3
Quebec 47 J7
Quebec (Prov.) 47 J6
Queen Charlotte Is. 46 C6
Queen Mary Land 59 G2
Queensland 55 G4
Queenstown 44 N10
Quetta 38 B2
Quezaltenango 50 F5
Quezon City 43 F3
Quimper 26 B3

Qui Nhon 42 C3
Quito 52 B3

R
Raba 42 E7
Rabat 44 D1
Rach Gla 42 C3
Radom 31 J3
Raipur 38 E4
Rajkot 38 C4
Raleigh 49 L4
Ramah 36 E4
Rampur 38 D3
Ramsgate 23 J5
Rancagua 53 B6
Ranchi 39 F4
Randers 29 F7
Rangoon 39 H5
Rantekombola 42 F6
Rarotonga 56 J9
Rasht 36 E2
Ratlam 38 D4
Rauma 29 H6
Ravenna 32 D2
Rawalpindi 38 C2
Razgrad 33 L3
Ré, Île de 26 D3
Reading 23 G5
Recife 52 F3
Red R. (USA) 49 G5
Red R. (Vietnam) 42 B1
Red Sea 36
Rea, Lough 25 C3
Regensburg 30 E4
Reggio 32 E5
Regina 46 F6
Reims 27 F2
Rennes 26 D2
Reno 48 C4
Resistencia 53 D5
Réthimnon 33 K7
Revilla Gigedo Is. 57 P5
Rey 37 F2
Reykjavik 29 A2
Reynosa 50 E2
Rezaiyeh 36 E2
Rhine 30 B3
Rhode Island 49 M3
Rhodes 33 M6
Rhodes (I.) 33 L6
Rhodope Mts. 33 J4
Rhondda 23 D5
Rhum 24 B4
Ribeirão Préto 53 E5
Richmond 49 L4
Riga 34 C4
Rijeka 32 E2
Rimini 32 D2
Rio Branco 52 C3
Rio de Janeiro 53 E5
Rio Grande 50 E2
Ripon 22 F3
Riyadh 36 E5
Roccella 32 F5
Rochdale 22 E3
Rochester 49 L3
Rockhampton 55 J4
Rocky Mts. 46
Rohtak 38 D3
Romania 33
Rome 32 D4
Rosa, Monte 32 A2
Rosario 53 C6
Roscommon 25 C3
Roscrea 25 D4
Roskilde 29 F7
Ross Dependency 59 M3

Ross Sea 59 M3
Rostock 30 E1
Rostov 34 C5
Rotherham 22 F3
Rotorua 55 O9
Rotterdam 30 A3
Roubaix 27 F1
Rouen 26 E2
Rovno 34 C4
Rub al Khali 36 E6
Rugby 23 F4
Rugby 23 F4
Runcorn 22 E3
Ruse 33 K3
Rwanda 45 G5
Ryazan 34 C4
Ryde 23 F6
Rysy 31 J4
Ryukyu Is. 41 L5
Rzeszów 31 K3

S
Saarbrücken 30 B4
Saaremaa 29 H7
Sabadell 28 H2
Sabah 42 E4
Sacramento 48 B4
Safi 44 D1
Sahara 44 E2
Saharan Atlas 44 E1
Saharanpur 38 D3
Sahiwal 38 C2
St. Albans 23 G5
St. Andrews 24 F4
St. Austell 23 C6
St. Brieuc 26 C2
St Christopher-Nevis
    See St Kitts-Nevis
St. Etienne 27 G4
St. George's Channel 23 A5
St. Helens 22 E3
St. Helens, Mt. 48 B2
St. Helier 26 C2
St. John 47 K7
St. Johns 47 L7
St. Kitts-Nevis 51 M4
St. Lawrence 47 K7
St. Lawrence, Gulf of 47 K7
St. Louis 49 H4
St. Lucia 51 M5
St. Malo 26 C2
St. Moritz 32 B1
St. Nazaire 26 C3
St. Paul 49 H3
St. Peter Port 23 E7
St. Pierre 47 L7
St. Polten 31 F4
St. Quentin 27 F2
St. Vincent 51 M5
Sakhalin 35 J4
Salala 37 F6
Salamanca 28 D2
Salekhard 34 E3
Salem (India) 38 D6
Salem (USA) 48 B3
Salerno 32 E4
Salisbury 23 F5
Salmon River Mts. 48 C3
Salta 53 C5
Saltillo 50 D2
Salt Lake City 48 D3
Salto 53 D6
Salvador 52 F4
Salzburg 30 E5
Salzgitter 30 D2
Samar 43 G3
Samarinda 42 E6
Samarkand 34 E6

89

Samoa 56 H8
Sámos 33 L6
Samothráki 33 K4
Samsun 36 C1
Sana 36 D6
San Ambrosio 53 B5
San Antonio 48 G6
San Bernardino 48 C5
San Cristóbal 52 B2
San Diego 48 C5
Sandringham 22 H4
San Felix 53 A5
San Fernando 52 C2
San Francisco 48 B4
San Jose (Costa Rica) 51 H6
San Jose (USA) 48 B4
San Juan (Argentina) 53 C6
San Juan (Puerto Rico) 51 L4
San Luis Potosi 50 D3
San Marino 32 D3
San Miguel 50 G5
San Miguel del Tucumán 53 C5
San Pablo 43 F3
San Pedro Sula 50 G4
San Salvador 50 G5
San Sebastian 28 F1
Santa Ana 50 G5
Santa Barbara 48 C5
Santa Clara 51 J3
Santa Cruz 52 C4
Santa Fe 48 E4
Santa Fé 53 C6
Santa María 53 D5
Santander 28 E1
Santarém 28 B3
Santiago (Chile) 53 B6
Santiago (Dom. Rep.) 51 K4
Santiago de Compostela 28 B1
Santiago de Cuba 51 J3
Santiago del Estero 53 C5
Santo André 53 E5
Santo Domingo 51 L4
Santos 53 E5
São Francisco 52 E4
São José do Rio Prêto 52 E5
São Luis 52 E3
Saône 27 G3
São Paulo 53 E5
São Tomé 44 E4
Sapporo 41 O2
Sarajevo 33 G3
Saratov 34 D4
Sarawak 42 D5
Sardinia 32 B4
Sargodha 38 C2
Sark 26 C2
Saskatchewan 46 F6
Saskatchewan R. 46 F6
Saskatoon 46 F6
Sássari 32 B4
Satu Mare 33 J1
Saudi Arabia 36
Sault Sainte Marie 47 H7
Sava 32 F2
Savannah 49 K5
Scafell Pike 22 D2
Scarborough 22 G2
Schwerin 30 D2
Scilly Is. 23 A7
Scotia Sea 59 T1
Scotland 24
Scunthorpe 22 G3
Seattle 48 B2
Segovia 28 D2
Seine 27 F2
Sekondi-Takoradi 44 D4
Selkirk Mts. 46 E6

Selvas 52 C3
Semarang 42 D7
Semipalatinsk 34 F4
Sendai 41 O3
Sénégal 44 C3
Senegal 44 C3
Senja 29 G5
Sennar 36 B7
Seoul 41 L3
Serov 34 E4
Sérrai 33 J4
Setúbal 28 B3
Severn 22 D4
Severnaya Zemlya 35 F2
Seville 28 D4
Seward 46 B4
Seydhisfjördhur 29 C2
Sfax 45 F1
Shah Fuladi 37 J3
Shahjahanpur 38 D3
Shanghai 41 K4
Shannon 25 D3
Shantar Is. 35 H4
Shantou 41 J6
Shaoyang 41 H5
Sharjah 37 G4
Sheffield 22 F3
Shëngjin 33 G4
Shenyang 41 K2
Shetland Is 24 A1
Shijiazhuang 41 H3
Shikoku 41 M4
Shilka 35 G4
Shin, Loch 24 D2
Shiraz 37 F4
Shizuoka 41 N4
Shkodër 33 G3
Shkodër, Lake 33 G3
Sholapur 38 D5
Shreveport 49 H5
Shrewsbury 22 E4
Shwebo 39 H4
Sialkot 38 C2
Siam, Gulf of 42 B3
Siauliai 29 H7
Siberut 42 A6
Sibu 42 D5
Sicily 32 D6
Sidi-bel-Abbès 44 D1
Siedlce 31 K2
Siegen 30 C3
Sierra Leone 44 C4
Sierra Madre Occidental 50 C2
Sierra Madre Oriental 50 E3
Sierra Morena 28 D3
Sierra Nevada (Spain) 28 E4
Sierra Nevada (USA) 48 C4
Siglufjördhur 29 B1
Siirt 36 D2
Silgarhi 38 E3
Silistra 33 L2
Simeulue 42 A5
Simferopol' 34 C5
Simpson Desert 54 F4
Sines 28 B4
Singapore 42 B5
Sining 40 F3
Sinop 38 C1
Sintang 42 D5
Sioux City 49 G3
Sioux Falls 49 G3
Siracusa 32 E6
Sisophon 42 B3
Sittwe 39 G4
Sivas 36 C2
Skagerrak 29 E7
Skagway 46 C5

Skegness 22 H3
Skellefteå 29 H6
Skíros 33 K5
Skopje 33 H3
Skye 24 B3
Slagelse 29 F7
Sligo 25 C2
Slough 23 G5
Smöla 29 E6
Smolyan 33 K4
Snaefell 22 C2
Snake 48 D3
Snåsa 29 F6
Snowdon 22 C3
Society Is. 57 L8
Sofia 33 J3
Sogne Fjord 29 E6
Söke 33 L6
Sokoto 44 E3
Solomon Is. 56 E7
Solway Firth 22 D2
Somali Republic 45 J4
Sombor 33 G2
Somerset I. 46 G2
Somme 27 F1
Songkhla 42 B4
Söröya 29 H4
Sortavala 29 K6
South Africa 44 M10
South America 52
Southampton 23 F6
Southampton I. 47 H4
South Atlantic Ocean 53 F6
South Australia 54 E5
South Carolina 49 K5
South China Sea 42 D3
South Dakota 48 F3
South Downs 23 G6
Southend 23 H5
Southern Alps 55 N10
Southern Ocean 59
Southern Uplands 24 D5
South Georgia 59 A1
South I. 55 N10
South Korea 41 L3
South Orkneys 59 T2
South Pacific Ocean 55 O10
South Pole 59
Southport 22 D3
South Shetlands 59 T2
South Shields 22 F2
South Uist 24 A3
South Yemen 36 E6
Soviet Union (See USSR)
Soweto 44 N9
Spain 28
Spalding 22 G4
Spencer Gulf 54 F7
Spey 24 E3
Spittal 32 D1
Split 32 F3
Spokane 48 C2
Spree 31 F3
Springfield (Ill., USA) 49 J4
Springfield (Mo., USA) 49 H4
Springs 44 N9
Spurn Head 22 H3
Sri Lanka 38 E7
Srinagar 38 C2
Strafford 32 C5
Stanley 53 D8
Stara Zagora 33 K3
Stargard 31 F2
Stavanger 29 E7
Stavropol' 34 D5
Stewart I. 55 M11
Stirling 24 E4

Stockholm 29 G7
Stockport 22 E3
Stockton-on-Tees 22 F2
Stoke-on-Trent 22 E3
Stonehaven 24 F4
Stonehenge 23 F5
Stornoway 24 B2
Strabane 25 D2
Strait of Dover 23 J6
Stralsund 30 E1
Stranraer 24 D6
Strasbourg 27 H2
Stratford-upon-Avon 23 F4
Stromeferry 24 C3
Stroud 23 E5
Struttgart 30 C4
Suakin 36 C6
Subotica 33 G1
Sucre 52 C4
Sudan 36 B6
Sudbury 47 H7
Sudeten Mts. 31 G3
Suez 36 B3
Suez, Gulf of 36 B4
Suez Canal 36 B3
Sukkur 38 B3
Sulaiman Range 38 B3
Sulawesi 42 F6
Sulu Sea 42 E4
Sumatra 42 B6
Sumba 42 E7
Sumbawa 42 E7
Sumy 34 C4
Sunderland 22 F2
Sundsvall 29 G6
Superior, Lake 29 J2
Surabaya 42 D7
Surakarta 42 D7
Surat 38 C4
Surinam 52 D2
Suzhou 41 K4
Svalbard 58 L3
Sverdlovsk 34 E4
Swains I. 56 H8
Swansea 23 D5
Swaziland 44 P9
Sweden 29
Swindon 23 F5
Switzerland 27
Sydney (Australia) 55 J6
Sydney (Canada) 47 K7
Syktyvkar 34 D3
Syracuse 49 L3
Syr Darya 34 E5
Syria 36 C2
Syrian Desert 36 C3
Szczecin 31 F2
Szeged 31 J5
Szombathely 31 G5

T
Tabora 45 H5
Tabriz 36 E2
Tabuk 36 C4
Tacoma 48 B2
Taegu 41 L3
Taejon 41 L3
Taganrog 34 C5
Tagus 28 C3
Tahiti 57 L8
Taibei 38 K5
Taichung 41 K6
Tainan 41 K6
Taiwan 41 K6
Taiyuan 41 H3
Taizz 36 D7

90

Tajrish 37 F2
Talaud Is. 43 G5
Talca 53 B6
Talcahuano 53 B6
Tallahassee 51 H1
Tallinn 34 C4
Tamale 44 D4
Tamar 23 C6
Tambov 34 D4
Tampa 51 H2
Tampere 29 H6
Tampico 50 E3
Tamworth (Australia) 55 J6
Tamworth (England) 22 F4
Tana 29 J5
Tanga 45 H5
Tanganyika, Lake 45 G5
Tangier 44 D1
Tangshan 41 J3
Tanimbar Is. 43 H7
Tanjungkarang 42 C7
Tanta 36 B3
Tanzania 45 H5
Tapachula 50 F5
Tapajós 52 D3
Tarancón 28 E2
Táranto 32 F4
Tarbert 24 B3
Tarbes 26 E5
Taree 55 J6
Tarnow 31 J3
Tarragona 28 G2
Tarrasa 28 G2
Tashkent 34 E5
Tasmania 55 H8
Tasman Sea 55 N10
Taunton 23 D5
Taupo 55 O9
Taupo, Lake 55 O9
Tauranga 55 O9
Taurus Mts. 36 B2
Tavoy 39 H6
Tawau 42 E5
Tay 24 E4
Tay, Loch 24 D4
Taymyr Peninsula 34 F2
Tbilisi 34 D5
Tees 22 F2
Tegucigalpa 50 G5
Tehran 37 F2
Teifi 23 C4
Tekirdag 33 L4
Tel-Aviv-Yafo 36 B3
Telford 22 E4
Temirtau 34 E4
Temuco 53 B6
Tennant Creek 54 E3
Tennessee 49 J4
Tennessee R. 49 J4
Tepic 50 D3
Tersina 52 E3
Terni 32 D3
Terre Adélie 59 J3
Tete 45 H6
Tetuan 44 D1
Texas 48 G5
Thailand 42 B2
Thames 23 F5
Thar Desert 38 C3
Tharthar Basin 36 D3
Thásos 33 K4
Thessaloniki 33 J4
Thimbu 49 F3
Thionville 27 H2
Thira 33 K6
Thunder Bay 47 H7
Thuringian Forest 30 D3

Thurles 25 D4
Thurso 24 E2
Tianjin 41 J3
Tiber 32 D3
Tibesti Mts. 45 F3
Tibetan Plateau 39 F2
Tierra del Fuego 53 C8
Tigris 36 D3
Tijuana 50 A1
Timaru 55 N10
Timbuktu 44 D3
Timisoara 33 H2
Timmins 47 H7
Timor 43 G7
Timor Sea 54 C2
Tinos 33 K6
Tipperary 25 C4
Tiranë 33 G4
Tiraspol 33 M1
Tiree 24 B4
Tirgu Mures 33 K1
Tirich Mir 37 K2
Tirsa 32 B4
Tiruchirapalli 38 D6
Tisza 31 J5
Titicaca, Lake 52 C4
Titograd 33 G3
Titov Veles 33 H4
Tlemcen 44 D1
Toamasina 45 J6
Toba, Lake 42 A5
Tobago 51 M5
Tobruk 45 G1
Tocantins 52 E3
Togo 44 E4
Tokelau 56 H7
Tokyo 41 N3
Tolbukhin 33 L3
Toledo (Spain) 28 D3
Toledo (USA) 49 K3
Toliara 45 J7
Toluca 50 E4
Tol'yatti 34 D4
Tomsk 34 F4
Tonga 56 H8
Tonghua 41 L2
Tonle Sap 42 B3
Toowoomba 55 J5
Topeka 49 G4
Torbay 23 D6
Töre 29 H5
Torne 29 H5
Toronto 47 J8
Torreón 50 D2
Torres Strait 43 K8
Tortosa 28 G2
Toruń 31 H2
Toulon 27 G5
Toulouse 26 E5
Tours 26 E3
Townsville 55 H3
Tralee 25 B4
Trang 42 A4
Transantarctic Mts. 59
Transylvanian Alps 33 J2
Trápani 32 D5
Trasimeno, Lake 32 D3
Trebon 31 F4
Trent 22 G3
Trieste 32 D2
Trikkala 33 H5
Trincomalee 38 E7
Trinidad 52 C1
Tripoli (Lebanon) 36 C3
Tripoli (Libya) 45 F1
Trivandrum 38 D7
Trois-Rivières 47 J7

Trollhättan 29 F7
Tromso 29 G5
Trondheim 29 F6
Trondheim Fjord 29 F6
Tropic of Cancer 57 M4
Tropic of Capricorn 57 N9
Troyes 27 G4
Trujillo 52 B3
Truro 23 B6
Tsumeb 45 F6
Tuamotu Archipelago 57 L8
Tubuai Is. 56 K9
Tucson 48 D5
Tukana, Lake 45 H4
Tula 34 C4
Tulcea 33 M2
Tulsa 49 G4
Tunbridge Wells 23 H5
Tunis 45 F1
Tunisia 45 E1
Tunja 52 B2
Turin 32 A2
Turkey 36 B2
Turks and Caicos Is. 51 K3
Turku 29 H6
Turnu Severin 33 J2
Tuscaloosa 49 J5
Tuticorin 38 D7
Tuvalu 56 G8
Tuxtla Gutiérrez 50 F4
Tuz, Lake 36 B2
Tuzla 33 G2
Tweed 24 F5
Tyne 22 E1
Tyrrhenian Sea 32 D5
Tyumen 34 E4
Tzekung 40 F5

U
Ubangi 45 G4
Uberaba 52 E4
Uberlândia 52 E4
Ubon Ratchathani 42 B2
Udaipur 38 C4
Udine 32 D1
Udon Thani 42 B2
Ufa 34 D4
Uganda 45 H4
Ujjain 38 D4
Ujung Pandang 42 E7
Ulan Bator 35 G5
Ulan-Ude 35 G4
Ullapool 24 C3
Ulm 30 C4
Ul'yanovsk 34 D4
Ume 29 G6
Umeå 29 H6
United Arab Emirates 37 F5
United Kingdom 20 C3
United States of America 48
Upington 44 M9
Upper Lough Erne 25 D2
Uppsala 29 G7
Ural 34 D5
Ural Mts. 34 D4
Ural'sk 34 D4
Urfa 36 C2
Urmia, Lake 36 E2
Uruguaiana 53 D5
Uruguay 53 D6
Urumchi 34 F5
USSR 34
Usti nad Labem 31 F3
Ust Urt Plateau 21 J4
Utah 48 D4
Utica 49 M3
Utrecht 30 A2

Uzhogrod 31 K4

V
Vaal 44 N9
Vaasa 29 H6
Vadodara 38 C4
Vaduz 30 C5
Váh 31 H4
Valdepeñas 28 E3
Valdivia 53 B6
Valence 27 G4
Valencia (Spain) 28 F3
Valencia (Venezuela) 52 C1
Valencia, Gulf of 28 G3
Valenciennes 27 F1
Valladolid 28 D2
Valledupar 52 B1
Valletta 32 E7
Valparaíso 53 B6
Van, Lake 36 D2
Vancouver 46 D7
Vancouver I. 46 D7
Vänern, Lake 29 F7
Vannes 26 C3
Vanuatu 56 F8
Varánasi 39 E3
Vardar 33 J4
Varna 33 L3
Västerås 29 G7
Vättern, Lake 29 F7
Växjö 29 F7
Vaygach 34 D2
Vega 29 F5
Venezuela 52 C2
Venice 32 D2
Venice, Gulf of 32 D2
Veracruz 50 E4
Vercelli 32 B2
Verdun 30 A4
Vereeniging 44 N9
Verkhoyansk Range 35 H3
Vermont 49 M3
Verona 32 C2
Versailles 27 F2
Vesterålen 29 F5
Vest Fjorden 29 F5
Vesuvius 32 E4
Vettore, Monte 32 D3
Vichy 27 F3
Victoria 55 G7
Victoria, Lake 45 H5
Victoria, Mt. 39 G4
Victoria I. 46 F2
Victoria Land 59 K3
Vidin 33 J3
Vienna 21 G4
Vientiane 42 B2
Vietnam 42 C2
Vignemale, Pic de 26 D5
Vigo 28 B1
Vijayawada 38 E5
Vikna 29 F6
Villach 32 D1
Villahermosa 50 F4
Villaputzu 32 B5
Vilnius 34 C4
Viña del Mar 53 B6
Vinh 42 C2
Vinnitsa 34 C5
Virginia 49 L4
Virgin Is. of the U.S. 51 M4
Virovitica 32 F2
Visby 29 G7
Viscount Melville 46 F2
Viso, Mt. 32 A2
Vishakhapatnam 39 E5
Vistula 31 J3

INDEX
TO
MAPS

INDEX TO FLAGS

INDEX TO FLAGS